SHEPHERD'S NOTES

SHEPHERD'S NOTES

When you need a guide through the Scriptures

Joshua, Judges

BROADMAN
&HOLMAN
PUBLISHERS

Nashville, Tennessee

© 1998

by Broadman & Holman Publishers

Nashville, Tennessee

All rights reserved

Printed in the United States of America

0–8054–9058–2

Dewey Decimal Classification: 222.20

Subject Heading: BIBLE. O.T. JOSHUA, JUDGES

Library of Congress Card Catalog Number: 97–32787

Library of Congress Cataloging-in-Publication Data

Joshua, Judges / Paul Wright, editor

    p. cm. — (Shepherd's notes)

    Includes bibliographical references.

    ISBN 0–8054–9058–2

    1. Bible. O.T. Joshua—Study and teaching. 2. Bible. O.T. Judges—Study and
teaching. I. Wright, Paul, 1955–. II. Series.

BS1295.5.J67   1998

222'.207—dc21

97–32787

CIP

1 2 3 4 5 6   03 02 01 00 99 98

CONTENTS

FOREWORD

Dear Reader:

Shepherd's Notes are designed to give you a quick, step-by-step over-view of every book of the Bible. They are not meant to be substitutes for the biblical text; rather, they are study guides intended to help you explore the wisdom of Scripture in personal or group study and to apply that wisdom successfully in your own life.

Shepherd's Notes guide you through the main themes of each book of the Bible and illuminate fascinating details through appropriate com-mentary and reference notes. Historical and cultural background information brings the Bible into sharper focus.

Six different icons, used throughout the series, call your attention to historical-cultural information, Old Testament and New Testament references, word pictures, unit summaries, and personal application for everyday life.

Whether you are a novice or a veteran at Bible study, I believe you will find *Shepherd's Notes* a resource that will take you to a new level in your mining and applying the riches of Scripture.

In Him,

David R. Shepherd
Editor-in-Chief

HOW TO USE THIS BOOK

DESIGNED FOR THE BUSY USER

Shepherd's Notes for Joshua and Judges is designed to provide an easy-to-use tool for getting a quick handle on these significant Bible books important features, and for gaining an understanding of their messages. Information available in more difficult-to-use reference works has been incorporated into the *Shepherd's Notes* format. This brings you the benefits of many advanced and expensive works packed into one small volume.

Shepherd's Notes are for laymen, pastors, teachers, small-group leaders and participants, as well as the classroom student. Enrich your personal study or quiet time. Shorten your class or small-group preparation time as you gain valuable insights into the truths of God's Word that you can pass along to your students or group members.

DESIGNED FOR QUICK ACCESS

Bible students with time constraints will especially appreciate the timesaving features built into the *Shepherd's Notes*. All features are intended to aid a quick and concise encounter with the heart of the messages of Joshua and Judges.

Concise Commentary. The books of Joshua and Judges are filled with action, adventure, and characters who respond to God's call in their lives. Short sections provide quick "snapshots" of the narrative and themes of these books, highlighting important points and other information.

Outlined Text. Comprehensive outlines cover the entire texts of Joshua and Judges. This is a valuable feature for following each narrative's flow, allowing for a quick, easy way to locate a particular passage.

Shepherd's Notes. These summary statements or capsule thoughts appear at the close of every key section of the narratives. While functioning in part as a quick summary, they also deliver the essence of the message presented in the sections which they cover.

Icons. Various icons in the margin highlight recurring themes in the books of Joshua and Judges aiding in selective searching or tracing of those themes.

Sidebars and Charts. These specially selected features provide additional background information to your study or preparation. Charts offer a quick overview of important subjects. Sidebars include definitions as well as cultural, historical, and biblical insights.

Maps. These are placed at appropriate places in the book to aid your understanding and study of a text or passage.

Questions to Guide Your Study. These thought-provoking questions and discussion starters are designed to encourage interaction with the truth and principles of God's Word.

DESIGNED TO WORK FOR YOU

Personal Study. Using the Shepherd's Notes with a passage of Scripture can enlighten your study and take it a new level. At your fingertips is information that would require searching several volumes to find. In addition, many points of application occur throughout the volume, contributing to personal growth.

Teaching. Outlines frame the texts of Joshua and Judges, providing a logical presentation of their messages. Capsule thoughts desginated as "Shepherd's Notes" provide summary statements for presenting the essence of key points and events. Application icons point out personal application of this messages of the books. Historical Context icons indicate where cultural and historical background information is supplied.

Group Study. Shepherd's Notes can be an excellent companion volume to use for gaining a quick but accurate understanding of the messages of Joshua and Judges. Each group member can benefit by having his or her own copy. The *Note's* format accommodates the study of themes throughout Joshua and Judges. Leaders may use its flexible features to prepare for group sessions or use them during group sessions. Questions to guide your study can spark discussion of Joshua and Judges' key points and truths to be discovered in these action books.

LIST OF MARGIN ICONS USED IN JOSHUA AND JUDGES

 Shepherd's Notes. Placed at the end of each section, a capsule statement provides the reader with the essence of the message of that section.

 Old Testament Reference. Used when the writer refers to Old Testament passages or when Old Testament passages illuminate a text.

 New Testament Reference. Used when the writer refers to New Testament passages that are either fulfilled prophecy, an antitype of an Old Testament type, or a New Testament text which in some other way illuminates the passages under discussion.

 Historical Context. To indicate historical information—historical, biographical, cultural—and provide insight on the understanding or interpretation of a passage.

 Personal Application. Used when the text provides a personal or universal application of truth.

 Word Picture. Indicates that the meaning of a specific word or phrase is illustrated so as to shed light on it.

JOSHUA
INTRODUCTION

Joshua is the first book in the section of the Old Testament commonly called the Books of History (Joshua–Esther).

In spite of its title, the book of Joshua is not a biography of Joshua, one of ancient Israel's most important leaders. Rather, the book tells the story of how God gave Israel, His chosen people, their own land, just as he had promised to do over four hundred years earlier (Gen. 15:15–21). While Joshua was Israel's leader during this time, the main character of the book, as is the case throughout the Bible, is God. With God directing events, the book of Joshua is optimistic about Israel's future in their new land. Joshua begins with a daunting challenge but ends with the quiet assurance that the task at hand, the conquest and settlement of Canaan, would be accomplished in full.

AUTHOR, AUDIENCE, AND DATE OF WRITING

There are more questions than answers regarding the authorship of Joshua. Because the book is anonymous, it is also impossible to pinpoint either the date which the book was written or the identity of its original readers.

Early Jewish and Christian tradition held that the book of Joshua was written by Joshua himself. This tradition is based on statements found in Joshua 8:32 and 24:26. However, these verses say only that Joshua wrote out certain things specifically relating to the covenant which God had made with Israel, not the entire book of Joshua as it is found in our Bibles.

1

Of the twelve spies who had entered Canaan, only Joshua and Caleb brought back a favorable report (Num. 13:1–14:38). Joshua was chosen and commissioned by God to lead Israel into Canaan after the death of Moses (Num. 27:15–23; Deut. 31:14–15, 23; 34:9)

While this traditional view remains a live option today, most instead prefer to hold that Joshua was written some time later in ancient Israel's history. The primary reason for this is that the story begun in Joshua is continued in Judges, 1 and 2 Samuel, and 1 and 2 Kings—books which together relate the history of ancient Israel from the conquest of their land to their exile from it in 586 B.C. Because these books share a similar outlook, they were evidently intended to be read as a single, continuous work.

Several clues within the book suggest that it was written some time before the reign of David, the first strong king of ancient Israel:

1. Joshua 6:25 indicates that Rahab, or at least her family, was still alive at the time of writing;
2. Joshua 15:63 notes that the Jebusites still lived in Jerusalem, while 2 Samuel 5:6–10 records that the Jebusites were driven out of Jerusalem by David; and
3. Joshua 16:10 states that the Canaanites still lived in Gezer, while 1 Kings 9:16 reports that the Canaanites were finally driven out of Gezer by Solomon, David's son and successor.

It is difficult to say how much of the book of Joshua was written "whole cloth" and how much was adopted from previous written sources.

One such source was the book of Jashar, an apparently older book referred to in Joshua 10:13 (cp. 2 Sam. 1:17–27) which recorded some of ancient Israel's heroic exploits in poetic form.

What is clear is that the process by which each biblical book was written—whatever its nature from a human point of view—took place under the guidance and direction of the Holy Spirit (2 Tim. 3:16). The book of Joshua is inspired Scripture, and its real author is God. Moreover, for purposes of the church, the audience of Joshua is us.

HISTORICAL CONTEXT OF THE EVENTS RECORDED IN JOSHUA

The conquest of Canaan by Israel under Joshua, as well as Israel's prior Exodus from Egypt under Moses, are usually dated by a variety of literary, historical, archaeological, and social scientific data. Most conservative Bible interpreters hold that Joshua lived in either the fifteenth or thirteenth centuries B.C. The evidence used to date these events is complex and largely inconclusive. Because scholars are divided in their interpretation of the evidence, including the evidence found within the Bible itself, it is best to leave the exact date open.

Nevertheless, the general historical and cultural setting of the events of Joshua is known. The polytheistic and nature-based fertility religion of the Canaanites was well established throughout the land into which Israel was entering. The main Canaanite deities were Baal, god of the thunderstorm, and his consorts Asherah (Judg. 6:25–32; 1 Kings 16:32–33; 2 Kings 17:16; 21:3) and the Ashtaroth (plural for "Ashtoret"; cp. Judg. 2:13; 10:6; 1 Sam. 7:4; 12:10). The Ashtaroth were a Canaanite form of Astarte, the common ancient Near Eastern goddess of love and fertility.

It is possible to derive a fairly complete picture of Joshua, Moses' successor, from the pages of Scripture. Joshua, who was a member of the Israelite tribe of Ephraim (Num. 13:8, 16), had been born in Egypt (cp. Exod. 33:11). As Moses' general (Exod. 17:8–13), he was present on Mount Sinai when God revealed the Law to Moses (Exod. 32:15–17). Joshua began his

This period, termed the Late Bronze Age by archaeologists and historians, was one that saw Egypt's long-standing influence in Canaan gradually decline. The hill country of Canaan, the area which Joshua was most able to conquer and hold, was generally sparsely settled. These rugged hills were home to several important city-states such as Hebron, Jerusalem (Jebus), Gibeon, Bethel, and Shechem, but their culture was not truly urban like the larger cities that dotted the coastal plain and large inland valleys.

career as the servant of Moses (Exod. 24:13: Josh. 1:1) but ended it, like Moses, as "the servant of the Lord" (Josh. 24:29: cp. 1:1)—sure testimony to his competence as a leader and his devotion to God.

PURPOSE

In the Hebrew Bible, the books of Joshua, Judges, 1 and 2 Samuel, and 1 and 2 Kings are together called the "Former Prophets" (the "Latter Prophets" are the books of Isaiah through Malachi, with the exception of the books of Daniel and Lamentations).

They were written to give hope to God's people—a people living under very real daily threats to their social, political, economic, and religious well-being—by reminding them of God's sure and active leadership in national and personal affairs. They were also written to confirm the warning of Moses (Deut. 28:1–68) that if God's people did not respond to Him with covenant loyalty, they would be uprooted from their land.

But there is more. Joshua centers on the fulfillment of the promise which God had made to the patriarchs Abraham, Isaac, and Jacob (Gen. 12:1; 13:14–15; 15:12–21; 26:3; 28:13; 35:12) and to Moses (Deut. 31:1–8, 23) that one day Israel would receive their own homeland. This promise was realized, at least in part, as Israel conquered Canaan under the leadership of Joshua.

God was faithful to His promise, and He would remain so. But His people, Israel, had a responsibility to respond faithfully to Him. Israel was to remain in their land as long as they kept the terms of the covenant which God had established with them and which He had revealed to them through Moses, primarily as recorded in the book of Deuteronomy (Josh. 22:5; 23:11; 24:14). The land, the place which God had specially prepared to be Israel's home, was a divine gift (24:13). But what God had given, He could also take away. The book of Joshua was written to teach Israel that God not only kept His promise to bring Israel back to their land after the long sojourn in Egypt, but that Israel had a responsibility to obey and serve God when they were settled there.

STRUCTURE AND CONTENT

The book of Joshua divides easily into three parts based on content: (1) Israel's entrance into Canaan, (2) the conquest of Canaan, and (3) the allotment of the land of Canaan to the twelve tribes of Israel.

LITERARY STYLE

Broadly speaking, Joshua is a narrative. That is, it tells a story with a unified plot and an overall cast of characters. The narrative of Joshua is composed of a number of separate episodes linked together with a common theme—the fulfillment of the covenant promise of land to Israel.

Joshua is also history, but not history written in the antiseptic, "just-the-facts, ma'am" way in which it is often thought to be written today. The history recorded in the book of Joshua is not an exhaustive account of all of the battles Israel fought to conquer Canaan. Rather, it is a selective retelling of certain important events, including some battles, recorded to proclaim God's view of why things happened the way they did. All of biblical history, in fact, is written with an eye toward God's underlying purposes for what sometimes seem to be merely random

Joshua was not written simply to provide ancient Israel with a record of events related to the conquest and settlement of Canaan. Rather, it spoke to the need of each Israelite to know who he was and where he belonged in a large and threatening world. He had a homeland, a place of "belonging to," where he could live in security and peace with his family, his people, and God.

The book of Joshua is part of the ongoing story of God's plan to redeem mankind.

(cp. 1 Kings 22:34) or humanly ordained (cp. 2 Kings 17:1–41) events.

THEOLOGY

Many foundational Biblical truths are proclaimed in the book of Joshua, such as:

- God is sovereign over people and nations (1:3; 5:13–15; 11:20; 23:3–5);
- God is faithful to His people and His promises (1:6; 21:43–45; 23:9–10);
- God's people are obligated to remain faithful to Him (1:7–8, 16–18; 22:5; 23:6–8; 24:14–15);
- God's people are bound together as a special community (7:1, 24–26; 24:25); and
- God wants His leaders to be righteous and courageous (1:1–9, 16; 11:23; 24:14–28).

The theological message of Joshua is grounded in the concept of covenant. The covenant which God established with the children of Israel at Mount Sinai bound Him and His people together in close relationship (Exod. 19:5–6). Israel was chosen by God to live in a land which He had specially prepared for them. They were expected to remain faithful to God alone (23:6–8, 11). If they failed to do so, they would not only cease to be prosperous and successful (1:8), but would "perish from this good land, which the Lord your God has given you" (23:13, 15–16; cp. 7:1–26). The choice to accept or reject God's will was made freely by each Israelite (24:14–24).

The book of Joshua is tied theologically to the books of the Pentateuch, in particular Genesis and Deuteronomy. The promises which God made in Genesis to the patriarchs—that they would become a strong and large nation in their own land (Gen. 12:1–3; 13:14–15; 15:12–21;

A covenant is a pact between two parties mutually binding them to certain agreed-upon obligations and benefits. Scripture refers to a number of covenants drawn up between various persons or nations. Covenants instituted by God include those made with Noah (Gen. 9:8–17), Abraham (Gen. 15:17–21; 17:2, 9–14), Moses (Exod. 19:5–6), David (2 Sam. 7:12–16; cp. 23:5), and the New Covenant of Jeremiah (Jer. 31:31–34). Although the form and details of these covenants differed, their basic content remained the same: "I shall be your God, you shall be my people, and I will dwell in your midst" (cp. Gen. 17:7; Exod. 6:6–7; 19:4–5).

26:3; 28:13; 35:12)—were fulfilled, at least in part, in the book of Joshua. Deuteronomy provided ancient Israel with a "constitution" for living in that land.

A difficult theological problem in Joshua is holy war. God commanded Joshua to completely destroy the Canaanites—men, women, and children—who lived in the land which Israel was entering (6:17, 21; 8:2; cp. Deut. 2:33–34; 3:3–6; 7:1–26; 20:16–18). Sometimes this was described by the phrase "to place under the ban" (6:17), indicating that the Canaanite cities, their inhabitants, and their wealth were to be completely burned and thereby given directly to God. Other times God instructed Joshua to kill the Canaanites *so that* Israel could take over their homes and land, and profit from them (1:15; 11:19–20, 23; 13:6; 23:4–5; 24:11–13; cp. Deut. 6:10–11).

The Bible offers several explanations for holy war: to reduce the threat of apostasy in Israel (Deut. 7:4–5, 25); to punish the Canaanites for their advanced state of sinfulness (Gen. 15:16; Deut. 9:4–5); and to provide a safe and secure home for Israel, the people whom God loved and had chosen for His own, special possession (Deut. 7:6–8; cp. Exod. 19:5–6; Mal. 1:2). Ultimately, however, it is the all-encompassing sovereignty of God, and this alone, that explains holy war (11:20).

THE MEANING OF JOSHUA FOR TODAY

The events recorded in the book of Joshua continue to hold meaning for Christians today, even though they took place half way around the world and over three thousand years ago. Because "all Scripture is . . . useful" for Christians (2 Tim. 3:16), it is important that

Although the call for holy war is difficult for Christians to understand, it must be accepted as appropriate for ancient Israel, given the time and circumstances of their founding. God's command to destroy the Canaanites was limited to a short period of Israel's history and in no way serves as a paradigm for Christian behavior today, except to underline the exclusive holiness demanded by God and to recognize that ultimately He is the victor over all sin.

Because God is sovereign in history, we can be sure that He is totally in control of the many circumstances of our lives. For example, because Joshua records how God controlled the outcome of battles between nations, we can know that He will also oversee the struggles which we face each day.

"By faith Abraham, when he was called, obeyed by going out to a place which he was to receive for an inheritance; and he went out, not knowing where he was going. By faith he lived as an alien in the land of promise, as in a foreign land, dwelling in tents with Isaac and Jacob, fellow heirs of the same promise; for he was looking for the city which has foundations, whose architect and builder is God" (Heb. 11: 8–10, NASB).

We stand as part of the same grand, ongoing story, each called at a specific time to a specific task and each provided with the opportunity to serve God in a special way (cp. 1 Cor. 12:4–7). Like Moses and Joshua, we must pass our faith in God and task in His kingdom on to others (Deut. 6:6–9; 2 Tim. 2:2).

believers strive to understand not just what Joshua says, but what it says *for us*.

Because the book of Joshua tells about the fulfillment of the promise of land to Israel, it has a built-in eschatological (or "end-times") character. The Promised Land which was given to Israel in the days of Joshua points to a "rest" to which Christians continue to look (11:23; cp. Deut. 12:9–10; Heb. 4:1–11). The Christian life parallels in part the "belongingness" which the land provided for ancient Israel. However, the full realization of the relationship which God intended for His people in the Promised Land will be found only in the heavenly Jerusalem (Heb. 11:8–10) and the new heaven and new earth written about by Isaiah (Isa. 65:17–25) and John (Rev. 21:1–22:5).

The book of Joshua also holds meaning for Christians because it speaks of effective leadership in challenging times. God chooses leaders appropriate to the time and task at hand, and His work goes on even after His servants, as indispensable as they may seem, pass on. Both Moses and Joshua were faithful to their calling and took care to hand what had been entrusted to them to a new generation (Deut. 31:1–29; 34:9; Josh. 1:1–18; 23:14–16; 24:14–28).

COVENANT MATTERS (1:1–18)

The book of Joshua begins where Deuteronomy leaves off, but the point of continuity is not simply chronological. The opening chapter of Joshua goes right to the heart of the matter. The responsibility for maintaining God's covenant stipulations and conquering the land promised to the patriarchs and Moses now fell on the shoulders of Joshua and the people he was about to lead into Canaan. Together, with the help of God, they could succeed.

GOD'S COMMISSION TO JOSHUA (1:1–9)

God had appointed Joshua to be Moses' successor while Moses was still alive (Deut. 31:1–8, 23; 34:9). Now that Moses was dead, God commissioned Joshua for the monumental task of leading Israel into Canaan. Joshua's commission involved three elements:

1. God first described the land which He was giving to Israel (1:2–4). His description corresponded to the land which had been promised to the patriarchs and Moses (Gen. 15:18; Exod. 23:31; Deut. 1:7; 11:24). Geographically, this region stretched from the Sinai Peninsula to the Euphrates River.

2. God then encouraged Joshua by assuring him that he would be successful in conquering the land (1:5–6). Three times God repeated the command: "Be strong and courageous" (1:6, 7, 9). Joshua could be confident because of God's promise, "I will never leave you nor forsake you" (1:5).

"Servant of the Lord"

In the Bible, the title "servant of the Lord" designated persons in special leadership roles who were obedient to God and to His covenant relationship. Moses was given the title (1:1; cp. Deut. 34:5), as was Joshua after a lifetime of service (24:24–29). Eventually, the prophet Isaiah used the title to refer to the coming Messiah (Isa. 42:1; 49:3; 52:13).

It was not until David that all of the land from the Sinai Peninsula to the Euphrates River came under Israelite hegemony. Even then the land from Damascus north was "Israelite" only in the sense that its local kings paid tribute to David and Solomon. Nevertheless, Joshua's work was considered complete (11:23) because it represented a *de facto* claim on the Promised Land.

3. Finally, God reminded Joshua that he must be careful to keep the covenant stipulations which Moses had written in the "Book of the Law" (1:7–9). As Moses had commanded Israel to place the words of God "upon [their] heart" (Deut. 6:6), so Joshua was told to "meditate on [them] day and night."

- *Joshua's responsibility to lead the people of*
- *Israel into Canaan, their Promised Land,*
- *was grounded in his careful obedience to*
- *God's commands and in God's faithfulness to*
- *the covenant promises.*

JOSHUA'S COMMISSION TO ISRAEL (1:10–18)

Joshua then began to prepare Israel to cross the Jordan River into Canaan. Israel was camped on the broad plains of Moab east of the Jordan River opposite Jericho. It was there that Moses had preached the sermons which make up the book of Deuteronomy—words of exhortation and instruction aimed specifically at helping the people of Israel meet the challenges of life once they were in their Promised Land (Deut. 1:5; cp. Num. 35:1; 36:13).

Joshua first commanded the Israelites to prepare themselves to cross the Jordan (1:10–11). He then asked the tribes who had received their landed inheritance east of the river—Reuben, Gad, and the half tribe of Manasseh—to remember Moses' instructions that before they settled down they must first help the other tribes conquer Canaan (1:12–15; cp. Num. 32:1–42; Deut. 3:12–22). Their response was wholehearted and enthusiastic: "Just as we fully obeyed Moses, so we will obey you" (1:17).

- *Joshua's first act of leadership was to rally*
- *his troops. Their favorable response was*
- *vital for the success of the mission. Everyone*
- *was focused on the future and God's upcom-*
- *ing blessing through them.*

QUESTIONS TO GUIDE YOUR STUDY

1. How does Joshua 1 help tie the Pentateuch to Israel's upcoming life in the Promised Land?
2. Based on chapter 1, characterize Joshua as a leader. What were his strengths? What might his weaknesses have been? See if your answer changes as you read the rest of the book.
3. Was the Israelite response in verse 17 realistic? How well did Israel obey Moses?

A change of leadership can be difficult, especially when the outgoing leader was both effective and highly regarded. God is in the habit of raising up people to do His work—and of seeing that His purposes continue to advance after they are gone. Moses' abilities were best suited for forging Israel into a nation in the wilderness, while Joshua was the best person to lead the conquest of Canaan. New leaders, when called by God, must be embraced for their own unique skills and, like Joshua, be given the chance to succeed.

ISRAEL'S ENTRANCE INTO CANAAN (2:1–4:24)

A prostitute's house was a place where people would come and go by night and not arouse undue suspicion (2:1).

Like the Exodus from Egypt, Israel's entrance into Canaan was accompanied by great miracles and acts of spiritual preparation.

SPYING OUT THE LAND (2:1–24)

Joshua began the conquest of Canaan by sending two spies into the land, reminiscent of Moses' actions almost forty years before (2:1; cp. Num. 13:1–33). This time, instead of being afraid of the Canaanites, the Canaanites were terrified of Israel (2:8–11).

Jericho is thought to be the oldest city on earth. Situated immediately opposite the plains of Moab and just six miles northwest of the Dead Sea, Jericho controlled the important trade route running the length of the Jordan Valley as well as access into the hill country of Canaan from the east. Fed by a spring at the foot of the city which still flows at the rate of one thousand gallons per minute, the region of Jericho is a veritable oasis in the arid Jordan Valley.

The spies hid overnight in Jericho in the house of a prostitute named Rahab. Rahab hid the spies from the king of Jericho, declaring to them that she had heard of the works of the Lord and knew that her city was doomed (2:3–11). Rahab then asked for mercy for herself and her family (2:12–14). After receiving assurances that her life would be spared, Rahab helped the spies escape (2:15–22). Their report to Joshua was optimistic, and it anticipated success—a far cry from the disbelieving report delivered by ten of the twelve spies (but not Joshua!) who had been sent out by Moses (2:23–24; cp. Num. 13:25–33).

■ *The spies' report sealed the doom of Jericho.*
■ *Nevertheless, Canaanites who chose to*
■ *believe in the Lord were given opportunity to*
■ *ally themselves with Israel and thus be saved*
■ *from the coming destruction.*

CROSSING THE JORDAN RIVER (3:1–17)

Joshua instructed his people to purify themselves in preparation for crossing the Jordan River. They were to be led by the Levitical priests who carried the ark of the covenant (3:1–3). The rest of the Israelites followed two thousand cubits—just over one-half mile—behind. This was a marked separation to show the holy presence of God among His people (3:4–6).

The entire procedure was first and foremost a religious act. Joshua told Israel that the priests were to lead so they would know "which way to go, since you have never been this way before" (3:4). The priests, custodians of Israel's spiritual heritage, thereby graphically portrayed their leadership role as teachers of the law—God's revealed "way" in which all Israel should walk (cp. Gen. 17:1; Deut. 5:33).

When the priests stood in the middle of the Jordan River at the very threshold of Canaan, the waters stopped flowing so that Israel could cross on dry ground (3:7–17). This event paralleled the crossing of the Red Sea, the threshold of Egypt, some forty years before (4:23; cp. Exod. 14:21–15:21). Then, Israel was delivered from Egyptian bondage; now they were being delivered from the wilderness to their ancestral home. In both cases, the biblical writers suggested that the waters parted because God marshaled the forces of nature to do His will: A strong east wind pushed back the waters of the Red Sea (Exod. 14:21), and a landslide blocked the Jordan upriver at Adam (3:15–16).

The books of Hebrews (11:31) and James (2:25) mention Rahab as a person who showed great faith in a difficult situation. Her denial to the king of Jericho (2:4–5) was a first step in turning from her pagan past to the Lord (cp. 2:11) and it should not be seen as condoning the seductive philosophy of "the ends justifies the means." At the very least, Rahab's actions showed that God works in unexpected ways, through human foibles and with people often considered to be the least likely to succeed.

Harvesttime in the land of Israel was in the spring, after the heavy winter rains had ceased and the flax, barley, and wheat matured. It was not unusual for the winding Jordan River, swelled by rainwater and melting snow from Mount Hermon, to undercut its soft marly banks. Evidently, this happened at Adam, a natural ford twelve miles north, just as the Israelites began to cross the river. The waters "rose up in a heap" behind the landslide which dammed the river, already rather shallow at this particular spot, until the pressure from behind cut a new channel so the river could continue to flow (cp. 4:18).

Several sites in the lower Jordan Valley have been suggested for the location of Gilgal but none is certain; the most popular lies just over a mile to the northeast of Jericho.

- *In reenacting the Exodus from Egypt while*
- *crossing into their new home, all Israel*
- *acknowledged the priority of God in their*
- *lives and their total dependence on Him.*

REMEMBERING THE MIGHTY ACTS OF GOD (4:1–24)

Joshua was concerned that the Israelites not only *do*, but that they *remember*. Looking to the past in order to become oriented to the present—and thereby gain confidence for the future—was an important element in ancient Israelite life (see Exod. 12:26–27; Deut. 6:20–24), as it is today in Judaism and should be in Christianity.

Joshua commanded twelve Israelites, one from each tribe, to pick up a large stone from the middle of the Jordan River and place them together in a heap (4:1–5). These stones were to be a permanent memorial testifying to future generations and the nations that Israel's entrance into Canaan was an act of divine favor (4:6–7; 21–24).

Israel crossed the Jordan River on the tenth day of Nisan, the first month in the Hebrew religious calendar (our March–April; 4:19). The twelve memorial stones were eventually erected in Gilgal (4:20; cp. v. 9), a site which became the military headquarters of Joshua during the Conquest (10:15) and remained an important religious center through the early Israelite monarchy (1 Sam. 7:16; 11:14–15; 13:4; 15:12, 21; 2 Kings 2:1).

■ By erecting memorial stones, Joshua pro-
■ vided a means by which Israel could remem-
■ ber that God had acted on their behalf. Thus,
■ they would be encouraged to remain faithful
■ to Him. The nations around Israel would
■ also learn of God from the stones' enduring
■ witness.

QUESTIONS TO GUIDE YOUR STUDY

1. How did Israel's entrance into Canaan under the leadership of Joshua differ from their attempted entrance described in Numbers 13–14?

2. In what ways did Joshua portray the crossing of the Jordan River as a religious event? Why did he do so?

3. Why is it important for Christians to remember the past?

Christianity is often characterized as a forward-looking religion, fixed on "the blessed hope—the glorious appearing of our great God and Savior, Christ Jesus" (Titus 2:13; cp. Eph. 1:18). It is important, however, that Christians also not forget to remember. The Lord's Supper was instituted by Jesus "In remembrance of me" (Luke 22:19; 1 Cor. 11:25). Numerous references in the New Testament to Old Testament characters and events (see Acts 7:1–53; Heb. 11:1–40; 1 Pet. 3:6) are intended to teach by remembering our common heritage with Israel.

ISRAEL'S CONQUEST OF CANAAN (5:1–12:24)

Joshua conducted three successive campaigns. The Israelites first pierced the center of Canaan, splitting the land in two. Joshua then defeated the major power centers in the south before turning to do battle against the strongest Canaanite city, Hazor, in the north. The writer of Joshua introduced each of these three campaigns—plus an intra-Canaanite flare-up recorded in chapter 9—with a statement summarizing the response of the Canaanite kings upon hearing of God's actions on behalf of Israel (5:1; 9:1; 10:1; 11:1). With the help of God, Joshua's brilliant military strategy opened up Canaan for Israelite settlement.

PUSHING INTO THE HEART OF CANAAN: THE CENTRAL CAMPAIGN (5:1–9:27)

Joshua's first campaign led Israel from Jericho in the Jordan Valley up to the plateau which controlled the most important crossroads in the hill country of Canaan. By pushing directly into the heart of Canaan, Joshua dealt his enemies a staggering blow.

Covenant Matters (5:1–15)

Upon hearing how Israel had crossed the Jordan River, the hearts of the kings of the Amorites and the kings of the Canaanites "melted, and they no longer had the courage to face the Israelites" (5:1). With such an introduction to the conquest narratives, the reader of Joshua can be sure of the outcome.

Before undertaking battle, Joshua was commanded by God to finish preparing the people for what was to be a holy war. Joshua first circumcised the men who had been born during Israel's period of wilderness wanderings (5:2–9).

Four days after crossing the Jordan River, Joshua led Israel in celebrating the Feast of Passover (5:10–11; cp. 4:19). Now that Israel was in Canaan, their Exodus and wilderness wanderings—a period of exile away from the Promised Land—was finally over. The freedom and deliverance marked by the first Passover was again realized (Exod. 12:1–51), and the manna, which had sustained Israel for a generation (Exod. 16:1–21), could stop (5:12).

On a lone reconnaissance around Jericho, Joshua had an experience similar to that of Moses before the burning bush (see Exod. 3:1–6). He was encountered by a mighty warrior whom he immediately recognized as an indispensable ally—or a formidable foe (5:13). The warrior, who was evidently an angel, refused to take sides in the upcoming battle but instead announced himself as the captain of the Lord's army (5:14). Joshua's response was one of complete obeisance (5:15).

■ *Although camped in their Promised Land,*
■ *Israel could not begin its conquest until they*
■ *were fully ready. They had to be totally sub-*
■ *mitted to God. This was more important than*
■ *mustering their military strength.*

The Conquest of Jericho (6:1–27)

The story of the conquest of Jericho is the most familiar event of the book of Joshua. The city's strategic location, dominating the lower Jordan

Circumcision, which had been initiated in Israel with Abraham (Gen. 17:9–14), signaled Israel's participation in God's eternal covenant. Because Abraham believed in God before he was circumcised (see Gen. 15:6), circumcision was intended from the beginning to be a sign of faith (cp. Deut. 10:16; 30:6).

In his initial question, "Are you for us, or for our enemies" (5:13), Joshua asked God to be on *his* side. By responding with a simple "Neither" (5:14), the divine warrior revealed that it was more proper for Joshua to volunteer to be on *God's* side. We should not ask God to bless our plans; rather, we ought to tell God that we are willing and available to be used in *His* plans.

Valley and routes into the hill country which lay beyond to the west, made its capture by Joshua crucial.

The conquest of Jericho has all the characteristics of a holy war. The battle was initiated at God's command (6:1–5), the attacking army was led by priests carrying the ark of the covenant (6:6–14), the offensive weapons—the sound of a trumpets (Hebrew *shofar*) and shouting by all the men of Israel—were effective only because of the intervention of God (6:15–20); and the city was "devoted . . . to the Lord" or placed under the ban (6:21).

The conquest of Jericho is often explained from a human point of view. Clearly, Joshua engaged in psychological warfare. On six successive days Jericho was circled in silence without attack; for the Canaanite king this must have been incomprehensible—and also maddening. Moreover, because Jericho sits within a rift valley demarcated by sizable fault lines, its destruction is often interpreted as having been caused by an earthquake. Nevertheless, the timing of the destruction—and the fact that it occurred at all—is testimony to God's power.

Joshua placed a curse on anyone who would rebuild Jericho (6:26–27). His curse was fulfilled in the days of Ahab, king of Israel, when the oldest and youngest sons of Hiel of Bethel lost their lives during the city's reconstruction (1 Kings 16:34).

■ With the destruction of Jericho, Joshua's con-
■ quest of Canaan had begun. Both Israel and
■ Canaan witnessed firsthand the power of
■ God. Success seemed inevitable.

The Hebrew term translated "under the ban" means "to devote" to God people or objects who are thoroughly hostile to Him. In some places, the term is translated "completely destroy" (see Deut. 2:34). The concept of the ban is related to the idea of holiness—total separation from things that are evil. By being placed "under the ban," a city and its inhabitants became God's exclusive property to dispose of as He saw fit. They were, in effect, offered up to Him as a burnt offering.

The Ai Affair (7:1–8:29)

The stunning victory at Jericho was followed by a defeat at Ai that left Israel reeling. God revealed that the cause of the defeat was the covenant unfaithfulness of Achan. After executing Achan and his family, Israel was able to conquer Ai.

The Defeat at Ai (7:1–5)

Joshua's next military objective was the city of Ai, located just below the strategic plateau which commands the crossroads of the hill country. By taking Ai, Joshua would gain a secure foothold in the heartland of Canaan and be able to position himself for an assault against the plateau which lay ahead.

However, chapter 7 opens with a foreboding note: Achan, from the tribe of Judah, had taken for his own use some things from Jericho which were supposed to have been placed under the ban. God was angered by this disobedience (7:1). Meanwhile Joshua, not knowing this, sent a small fighting force to attack Ai, because his spies had told him that the city could be easily taken (7:2–4). What should have been an easy victory was a shocking defeat instead (7:5).

It is difficult to corroborate the biblical story of the conquest of Jericho from the archaeological excavations. The site is highly eroded, and material evidence of settlement from the time of Joshua is meager. Nothing of the walls of Jericho from the time of the Israelite conquest remains; unfortunately, earlier claims to have found Joshua's walls was a result of misinterpretation of the evidence. There is a gap in settlement at Jericho following its conquest by Joshua which corresponds well to the biblical account of the ban placed on the city and the subsequent rebuilding of Jericho by Hiel of Bethel.

■ *The defeat at Ai showed that God's blessings*
■ *are not automatic. The privilege of being one*
■ *of God's people carries the responsibility of*
■ *living according to His high standards of*
■ *righteousness.*

The Sin and Punishment of Achan (7:6–26)

The defeat at Ai was greatly demoralizing, and Joshua's demeanor resembled that of Israel during its trying days in the wilderness (7:6–8; cp. Exod. 16:2–3; 17:3). Joshua pleaded with God for understanding, reminding Him that if Israel now failed in its conquest of Canaan, God's reputation (lit., "name") among the nations would be destroyed (7:9; cp. Num. 14:13–19; Deut. 9:25–29; Ezek. 36:22–36).

God finally revealed to Joshua what the reader of the story had suspected all along—that the defeat happened because "Israel has sinned" (7:11; cp. v. 1). The ban placed on Jericho required that all of its spoils be burned in God's presence and hence be given directly to Him. Instead, "they" (note the plural pronoun—7:11) sought to profit at God's expense—a flagrant and inexcusable violation of the covenant. By taking some of the wealth of Jericho, Achan put God's blessing of Israel in jeopardy. The actions of one affected the welfare of all.

God's solution was to have all Israel consecrate themselves and then appear before Him by tribes, families, households, and individuals, so that He could reveal the guilty party and thereby save everyone else (7:13–15). His finger fell on Achan, a man from the tribe of Judah, who readily confessed his wrongdoing (7:16–21). All

Israel, once implicated in the crime, now participated in the punishment. Achan, his family, and all his possessions were stoned and burned with fire, thereby being placed, like Jericho, under the ban (7:22–25).

Because of the intimate nature of life in an ancient Near Eastern tent, Achan's family must have participated in—or at least given acquiescence to—his crime, and so were also deserving of punishment under the spirit of the Israelite law. Joshua raised a pile of stones over Achan as a permanent reminder to Israel of Achan's unfaithfulness (7:26; cp. 4:19–24).

■ *Israel was called to a special kind of commu-*
■ *nity, where each person was devoted to God*
■ *but also to the ultimate good of each other.*
■ *By making the punishment of Achan a public*
■ *event, God sought to teach Israel the corpo-*
■ *rate ramifications of His covenant.*

The Conquest of Ai (8:1–29)

Having taken care of the sin in their midst, Joshua was now able to conquer Ai. God encouraged him not to fear or be dismayed (8:1). These words echoed His commission in chapter 1 and assured Joshua that the covenant promises still remained in effect.

The present topography surrounding the ancient site of Ai matches well the detailed description of the terrain recorded in Joshua 8, providing a valuable resource in reconstructing Joshua's campaign. Joshua set an ambush behind Ai, opposite the direction of his expected advance on the city (8:3–9). The next morning, when the sun was in the eyes of his

A key biblical concept that helps us understand the story of Achan is "group solidarity." In biblical culture, the connection between an individual and the social group(s) to which he belonged was much tighter than in the modern West. This is still true in many places in the world today. Because they were a covenant people, ancient Israel possessed a kind of "corporate identity" which meant that certain rights and responsibilities were incumbent on each individual for the good of the whole. A wrong committed against God by one person was tantamount to a wrong committed against God by all, and the entire group was responsible for the misdeeds of one of its members.

Taken from *Holman Bible Handbook,* (Nashville, Tenn.: Holman Bible
Publishers, 1992), 198.

enemy, Joshua attacked with a small force (8:10–14). He drew out the king of Ai by pretending to be beaten before him, thus allowing the ambush to sweep in from the rear and burn the city (8:15–20). Joshua's troops then fell back on the confused Canaanites to ensure complete victory (8:21–25). Like Jericho, all the inhabitants of Ai were killed and the city was burned with fire, but this time the Israelites were allowed to take spoil from the city for themselves (8:26–29).

■ *Having accepted the consequences of their*
■ *disobedience, the Israelites were able to con-*
■ *tinue with their conquest of the Promised*
■ *Land. The defeat of Ai enabled Israel to*
■ *secure a firm hold in the hill country of*
■ *Canaan.*

Covenant Matters (8:30–9:27)

The two episodes which followed the affair at Ai focused specifically on covenants. In the first, Joshua ratified the covenant between God and Israel according to the instructions given by Moses. In the second, Joshua was duped into establishing a covenant with Gibeon, the Canaanite city dominating the crossroads of the hill country.

The Covenant at Mounts Ebal and Gerizim (8:30–35)

After establishing an Israelite presence in the hill country of Canaan, Joshua turned north, to Mounts Ebal and Gerazim, to ratify God's covenant with His people. Nestled between these prominent hills lay the powerful Canaanite city of Shechem. Joshua would apportion this entire

The lack of clear archaeological remains dating to the time of Joshua at the ancient site of Ai is a long-standing point of contention in biblical studies. Many suggest that Ai was used as a military outpost for Bethel, a strong Canaanite city located at the crest of the hill country two miles west (cp. 8:17). This is consistent with the spy's report which mentioned that only a few people lived in Ai (7:3). The name *Ai* means "ruin" and refers to the ruins of a much earlier city at the site which were evident in Joshua's day. The "city" mentioned in Joshua 8:19 could refer to the remains at Ai, or the city of Bethel.

Shechem figured prominently in the stories of the patriarchs, especially Jacob, who had settled there (Gen. 33:18–34:31; cp. 12:6). There is no record of an Israelite conquest of Shechem or of the entire region between Bethel and the Jezreel Valley in the book of Joshua. It is possible that some of the citizens of Shechem welcomed Joshua and the Israelites as returning "citizens" of their town, thereby negating the need for conquest.

Archaeologists have uncovered a structure on Mount Ebal which is thought by some to be the altar which Joshua built for the covenant renewal ceremony.

region from Bethel to the Jezreel Valley (Plain of Esdraelon), with Shechem at its center, to the tribes of Ephraim and Manasseh eventually (16:1–17:18).

Joshua built an altar on Mount Ebal according to the prescription of Moses. Here he ratified the covenant as Moses had instructed him to do (8:31; cp. Exod. 20:25–26; Deut. 27:1–8). Joshua wrote "a copy of the law of Moses," probably the Ten Commandments, on stones erected on the site (8:32). Half of the Israelites stood on Mount Ebal and the other half on Mount Gerazim, reciting the blessings and curses which would befall them depending on their loyalty to the terms of the covenant (8:33; cp. Deut. 27:11–26). Joshua ended the ceremony by reading the entire law which God had revealed to Israel through Moses (8:34–35).

■ *At Jericho and Ai, God had proven faithful to*
■ *His covenant promises. Now all Israel*
■ *pledged their loyalty to Him by ratifying the*
■ *covenant.*

The Covenant with Gibeon (9:1–27)

With the fall of Ai, the Canaanite kings who lived in the hill country, in the foothills (Heb. *shephelah*; lit. "lowland") to the west, and on the Mediterranean coast knew their cities would also fall to Joshua. They responded by forming a coalition to fight against Israel (9:1–2).

The men of Gibeon, the city which controlled the strategic crossroads that lay next in Joshua's line of attack, realized more than the other Canaanites that defeat was inevitable. In desperation, they, along with three allied villages, tricked Joshua into entering into a covenant relationship with them (9:3–15). This act was a gamble, because the Gibeonites evidently knew that Israel was only supposed to enter into a covenant with God (hence they used a ruse). But they also trusted that Israel would remain faithful to their covenant partners regardless of the circumstances.

Upon learning of the ruse, the Israelites let Joshua know their dissatisfaction with his leadership abilities (9:16–18). Joshua was bound to keep the covenant and let the Gibeonites live in peace (cp. 2 Sam. 21:1–9), but he relegated them to a servant role (9:23; *servant* is better than "slave," KJV) within Israelite society. The Gibeonites and their descendants were given the task of supplying wood and water, two commodities necessary for sacrifice, for the ongoing Israelite religious ceremonies "at the place the LORD would choose" (9:19–21, 27). Realizing that this arrangement at least allowed them to live, the Gibeonites readily agreed.

It is often supposed that the role of "hewers of wood and drawers of water" was menial and degrading, and that by giving this job to the Gibeonites Joshua was consigning them to be second-class citizens in Israel. This is not necessarily so. Temples throughout the ancient Near East were wealthy institutions which employed vast numbers of people with a variety of skills, including craftsmen, farmers, merchants, and other workers of all sorts. Such jobs were in high demand among the general population because they provided an important degree of economic security in an otherwise harsh world. By serving in the temple, the Gibeonites were given an important role in Israelite society.

The "place the Lord your God will choose," a favorite phrase of Moses in the book of Deuteronomy (see Deut. 12:5, 11, 14, 18, 26), ended up being Jerusalem, but not until the time of David and Solomon. Before that time, the ark of the covenant, the focal point of Israelite worship, was located in several places, including Bethel (Judg. 20:18, 27), Shiloh (see Josh. 18:1; 1 Sam. 1:3) and Kiriath Jearim (1 Sam. 6:21–7:2). Appropriately, Kiriath Jearim was one of the cities whose men became "wood cutters and water carriers" under the covenant between Israel and Gibeon (9:17, 27).

The people of Gibeon—Canaanites who had not experienced the Exodus from Egypt or heard firsthand the revelation of God at Mount Sinai—thus became one with God's covenant people. God honored their ruse—or was it resourcefulness?—much as He had honored the faith of Rahab. Both instances show the inclusive nature of the Israelite faith. They were down payments on God's promise to bless the nations through Israel (Gen. 12:3).

It would be a mistake to conclude from Joshua's treatment of the Gibeonites that God condones a type of social stratification which leads to degrading an entire element of society. The Gibeonites became "hewers of wood and drawers of water," not because of their ethnic makeup or any other inherent characteristic but because they had deceived Joshua.

■ *With the subjugation of Gibeon—this time*
■ *through peace rather than warfare—Joshua*
■ *had split Canaan in two. Joshua remained*
■ *faithful to his covenant promise with Gibeon*
■ *even though the Gibeonites did not deserve it,*
■ *just as God continued to remain faithful to*
■ *His covenant promises with Israel.*

CUTTING OFF THE FEET OF CANAAN: THE SOUTHERN CAMPAIGN (10:1–43)

After dividing Canaan in two, Joshua set about to conquer the cities to the south and west of Gibeon. By defeating the major population centers throughout the region, Joshua was able to knock the feet out from under the Canaanites.

The Battle at Gibeon (10:1–15)

Jerusalem, the future capital city of Israel (cp. 2 Sam. 5:6–10), lay a short distance to the south of Gibeon. With his northern neighbors now allies of Israel, Adoni-zedek the king of Jerusalem was forced into action. He concluded an alliance with the kings of four other powerful Canaanite cities which were strategically located in the hills to the south and west—Hebron, Jarmuth, Lachish, and Eglon—and with them led an attack on the renegade Gibeon (10:1–5).

Joshua, faithful to his covenant with Gibeon, came to the aid of the Gibeonites. He marched his army all night from Gilgal in the Jordan Valley to the heights around Gibeon, a climb of 3,600 feet in 18 rugged miles. With the sun rising at his back and shining squarely into his enemies' eyes, Joshua attacked the Canaanite coalition "suddenly" (10:6–9). His stratagem caught the Canaanites totally by surprise, and the victory was complete. Joshua chased the Canaanites down the ascent of Beth-horon, the best natural route into the hill country from the west, to Azekah and Makkedah, cities in the western foothills (*shephelah*) which guarded important entrances to Jerusalem and Hebron (10:10). Once again, Joshua was careful to attack and defeat cities which were crucial for securing a stranglehold on the entire land.

The writer of Joshua was careful to describe the Israelite victory as a complete rout. Israel won because God turned the forces of nature—the very land which Israel was set to conquer—against the Canaanites (10:11–15; cp. Judg. 5:20–21).

Scholars have puzzled over the "long day" of Joshua 10:12–14. Some hold it to have been an eclipse accompanied by a hailstorm. Others suggest that unusual conditions in the atmosphere refracted the light of the setting sun to prolong the daylight. Still others declare the day to have been lengthened by a unique act of God, just as the star of Bethlehem was a unique sign for a unique event. Regardless of the explanation, the point of the story is that God, acting in His time and by His chosen means, gave the victory to His people (10:14).

■ *By defeating the coalition of southern kings,*
■ *Joshua claimed control over southern*
■ *Canaan. The strength of his army was*
■ *important for the fight, but the battle was*
■ *won only through the intervention of God.*

Mopping-up operations (10:16–43)

The Canaanite kings which had initiated the battle at Gibeon fled for their lives (10:16). Joshua's men caught up with them at Makkedah, where they hid in a cave (10:17–18). Joshua sent his army to capture their cities, then executed them according to the terms of execution set forth in Deuteronomy 21:22–23.

Chapter 10 concludes with a roster of battles which Joshua fought in southern Canaan, the territory which he would allot to the tribe of Judah (10:29–43; cp. 14:1–15:63). This listing gives brief attention to each battle, perhaps a

Some of the cities mentioned in Joshua 10 have been excavated by archaeologists. While their material remains vary, many show evidence of having been destroyed in the mid-thirteenth century B.C. Above these destruction layers were found small, poorer settlements, just the kind which would be expected from a seminomadic population such as Israel that was beginning to settle down in a new land.

literary technique to reflect a lightning campaign. The cities listed as destroyed by Joshua all controlled important valleys leading into Canaan from the west (for example, Lachish and Gezer), or strategic crossroads in the hill country (for example, Debir and Hebron, the latter a city where Abraham, Sarah, Isaac, Rebekah, and Jacob were buried). By taking these cities, Joshua sought to surround and isolate Canaan, thereby claiming the entire land for Israel. The summary statement recorded in verses 40–42 reflects the effectiveness of his plan. Later conquests were needed and, in fact, continued for generations, but the basic claim on central and southern Canaan was made by Joshua (cp. Josh. 15:14–19; Judg. 1:10–20; 2 Sam. 5:6–10).

■ *The writer of Joshua took care to provide*
■ *enough information about Joshua's conquest*
■ *of southern Canaan to ensure later genera-*
■ *tions that the land of Judah, from which the*
■ *messianic line would come, belonged*
■ *firmly—and only—to Israel.*

SMASHING THE HEAD OF CANAAN: THE NORTHERN CAMPAIGN (11:1–15)

The report of Joshua's final conquest, like the previous two, begins with a Canaanite response to the power of Israel and their God. Jabin, king of Hazor, "the head of all these kingdoms" (11:10), formed a mighty coalition of kings from across northern Canaan—a force apparently stronger than anything Joshua had yet faced (11:1–5). Hazor lay at the edge of the Huleh Valley, the extension of the Rift Valley north of the Sea of Galilee, and was the main city guarding the international route that entered Canaan from the north and east. Jabin gathered his combined forces at the waters of Merom, high in the hills of upper Galilee above Hazor, where he could avoid detection by Joshua's spies.

Joshua was not intimidated. He "came against [Jabin's army] suddenly at the Waters of Merom and attacked them" (11:6–7). The Canaanites, surprised that Joshua would attack their rugged "home court," were routed and Hazor was burned (11:8–15). Again, the writer of Joshua was careful to attribute Israel's victory to God's intervention and the obedience of Joshua (11:6, 8, 15).

■ *With the destruction of Hazor and the defeat*
■ *of the northern coalition, Joshua's work in*
■ *conquering Canaan was essentially com-*
■ *plete. He had done everything that the Lord*
■ *and Moses had told him to do.*

A SUMMARY OF JOSHUA'S VICTORIES IN CANAAN (11:16–12:24)

The conquest narratives end with a description of the land conquered by Joshua and a roster of conquered kings.

The description of the conquered land in Joshua 11:16–17 lists major geographical regions of Canaan from the far south (the Negev and Mount Halak) to the far north (Baal-gad in Lebanon at the foot of Mount Hermon). This was essentially the same region which Joshua would apportion to the tribes of Israel (11:23), and it became the land normally controlled by the kingdoms of Israel and Judah during the monarchy. However, it remained less than the entire

Ongoing archaeological excavations at the city of Hazor have substantiated the Bible's claim that Hazor "had been the head of all these kingdoms" (11:10). At two hundred acres in size, the walled city of Hazor in Joshua's day was more than ten times larger than any other Canaanite city and probably held thirty thousand people. Written documents from antiquity connect Hazor to the cities of Mesopotamia through the trade of tin, a commodity necessary in the manufacture of bronze. Recent excavations have uncovered the magnificent Canaanite palace located at the highest spot of Hazor, and testify to its destruction by an intense fire.

land which God had promised to Abraham (see Gen. 15:18).

Evidently, the writer of Joshua included only a partial record of Joshua's battles of conquest in chapters 5–11, for he noted in the end that "Joshua waged war against all these kings a long time" (11:18). With Joshua's march through Canaan, the land had been claimed for Israel. The "mopping-up" operations, some of which are alluded to in Joshua 11:21–22, would continue for generations. The conquest of Canaan was not considered complete until the conquests of David (2 Sam. 5:6–10; 8:1–18; 10:1–19; 24:1–9), a fact which made him the paradigm of an effective, anointed king to later generations (cp. 2 Sam. 23:1–7).

Joshua 12 contains a list of kings conquered by Israel. Those kings fall into three groups:

1. Kings conquered by Moses while Israel was still east of the Jordan. These include Sihon and Og (12:2–6; cp. Num. 21:21–35; Deut. 2:26–3:11).
2. Kings conquered by Joshua. These are listed in the same order in which they appear in the narratives of chapters 5–11, but not all kings encountered there (for example, Lachish, 10:31) are found in the list of Joshua 12.
3. Kings not specifically mentioned in the narratives of Joshua 5–11. Most of these kings controlled cities located in the major inland valleys of Canaan (for example, Taanach, Megiddo, and Jokneam) and along the Mediterranean sea coast (for example, Apheq and Hepher). Because these cities correspond to those which Israel was unable to conquer

according to Joshua 13:2–5 and Judges 1:27–33, some interpreters hold that the entire list either reflects the time of the conquests of David or is an idealized picture of the work of Joshua.

■ *Although the description of the conquered*
■ *land and the list of conquered kings present*
■ *some difficulties, they are clearly intended to*
■ *mark a turning point in the book of Joshua.*
■ *The land was claimed for Israel as God had*
■ *commanded; now it could be apportioned*
■ *among the various tribes.*

QUESTIONS TO GUIDE YOUR STUDY

1. What was the key factor in both the victories and the losses by Israel as they moved to possess Canaan?

2. How did Joshua use the physical features of the land to his own advantage in planning strategy and fighting battles against the Canaanites?

3. Explain how the writer of the book of Joshua used the concept of covenant to tie the various battle campaigns together.

As an explanation for Joshua's conquests, the writer included a note that God chose to destroy the Canaanites by hardening their hearts much as he had done to Pharaoh in preparation for the Exodus from Egypt (11:20; cp. Exod. 9:12; 14:17). God hardened Pharaoh's heart only after Pharaoh had first hardened his own heart (Exod. 8:32; 9:7, 12), and it can be assumed by the reader of Judges that the Canaanites had done the same thing. While God's grace is long-suffering, there comes a time when He no longer can tolerate the advance of sin in the lives of people.

The fourth major section of the book of Joshua is devoted to a careful delineation of the territories allotted to each tribe of Israel. Typically, these allotments appear as either border descriptions or city lists. Most of the geographical names included in Joshua 13–21 are unfamiliar to Bible readers, and the location of some are unknown even to scholars. A good Bible atlas is indispensable for a detailed study of these chapters.

Four of the nine chapters recording the division of the land in Joshua are devoted to Judah, Ephraim, and Manasseh. This emphasis must be understood in light of later biblical history, for it was their territorial allotments which became the heartland of the kingdoms of Judah and Israel.

GOD'S COMMISSION TO JOSHUA (13:1–7)

Joshua had grown old (13:1). His job in conquering the land of Canaan was over; it was now time to divvy up the spoils.

Although he laid claim to the whole land (cp. 11:23), Joshua was not able physically to conquer it all. Most of the land which remained to be conquered lay in the interior valleys and along the coast (13:2–5), but there remained pockets of resistance in the hill country as well (13:6). While God had promised to continue to aid Israel in acquiring the *entire* land, He commissioned Joshua to proceed with its apportionment as if the entire land already belonged to Israel (13:6–7).

■ *Joshua's job was not done until he had left a*
■ *lasting legacy to Israel: a place for each tribe*
■ *and family to settle down and call home.*

THE LANDS ALLOTTED BY MOSES IN TRANSJORDAN (13:8–33)

Before proceeding with an account of the division of the land, the writer of Joshua reviewed the allotment of lands in Transjordan to the tribes of Reuben and Gad and the half-tribe of Manasseh (13:8 13; cp. Deut. 3:12–17). Moses had given Reuben and Gad land which was taken from Sihon, king of the Amorites (13:15–28). This land was particularly well suited to cattle grazing, the economic basis of these tribes (see Num. 32:1–5). Jair and Makir, two clans from the tribe of Manasseh (hence the designation "half-tribe of Manasseh"; cp. 1 Chr. 2:21–23), had received the land which belonged to Og, king of Bashan (13:29–31).

Both Moses (Deut. 3:18–20) and Joshua (1:10–18) had made sure that Reuben, Gad, and the half-tribe of Manasseh remembered their responsibility to aid the other Israelite tribes in conquering the land west of the Jordan River.

■ *By reviewing the apportionment of Transjor-*
■ *dan before proceeding with the division of*
■ *Canaan, the writer of Joshua was able to give*
■ *a complete account of Israel's inheritance in*
■ *the Promised Land.*

God calls us to forge ahead in life. We may not feel as though we are ready to move on to greater challenges and areas of responsibility, or we many be satisfied in the security of the known. When He asks us to take a risk, we can be sure He has prepared the way in advance.

The homeland of Reuben and Gad was sandwiched between the countries of Moab to the south, Ammon to the east and Israel proper, which lay across the Jordan River, to the west. The half-tribe of Manasseh eventually bordered Syria. The entire area of Israelite settlement in Transjordan was thus a "land between" and was fought over throughout Old Testament history.

THE ALLOTMENT TO THE TRIBE OF JUDAH (14:1–15:63)

With the writer's attention now focused on the land of Canaan, the first mentioned inheritance naturally belonged to the tribe of Judah. Judah no doubt received pride of place because of its dominant role in later Israelite history.

Caleb's Request (14:1–15)

Joshua and Caleb were old friends. Years before, they alone among the twelve spies whom Moses had sent into Canaan brought back a favorable report of their ability to conquer the land (Num. 13:1–33). Because of their faith, God had allowed Joshua and Caleb to survive forty years in the wilderness and to enter the Promised Land (Num. 14:30). Now in the twilight of his career, Caleb approached Joshua in Gilgal and asked that he be given the very region of the hill country which had so terrified his fellow spies, for "the LORD helping me, I will drive them out just as he said" (14:1–12).

Joshua, no doubt impressed with Caleb's courage (see 1:6), granted him the city of Hebron, the most important population center in the southern hill country (14:13–15). Later Caleb would conquer a second city, Debir, located ten miles south of Hebron (15:13–19; see Judg. 1:11–15).

Caleb, the chosen representative for the tribe of Judah in the story of the spies (Num. 13:6) and the inheritor of Hebron, the city of the patriarchs, wasn't even a descendant of Israel. Caleb was a Kenizite (14:6), a member of a tribal group that had descended from Esau (Gen. 15:19; 36:9–11). The Kenizites were one of a number of groups that were absorbed by Judah during the early history of ancient Israel. Together they represent the inclusive nature of God's people.

■ *The mention of Caleb at the beginning of the*
■ *division of Canaan among the tribes signals*
■ *the ability of God to fulfill His promises.*
■ *Caleb not only remained alive to receive his*
■ *promised inheritance; he was willing to do*
■ *the work of a young man to get it.*

The Territory of Judah (15:1–12)

The territory of the tribe of Judah was delineated by both a border description (15:1–12) and a detailed city list (15:20–63).

The border of Judah encircled the southern Canaanite hill country, the lowlands (*shephelah*) and coast to the west, and the arid Negev to the south. Several points arise from this description which are important for later biblical history:

1. In the south, Judah was given territory which stretched half way to the Gulf of Aqaba (15:2–4), a largely empty region that carried camel caravans between Egypt and Edom. Largely for this reason, Judah was in perpetual conflict with its neighbors over this area.

2. To the west Judah was given all the land to the Mediterranean coast, a region which included the territory that was also being claimed by the Philistines (see 11:22). Conflicts with the Philistines defined Israel's political priorities throughout the time of the judges and its early monarchy (cp. Judg. 13–16; 1 Sam. 4–7; 13–14; 17).

3. The border description became very detailed in the vicinity of Jerusalem, a Canaanite (Jebusite) enclave just inside their northern border of Judah (15:7–9). Because Jerusalem was to become the capital of Israel, the hill country in its vicinity received special attention.

Othniel went on to become the first judge (lit., "deliverer") of Israel, freeing Israel from the oppression of Cushan-Rishathaim, king of Mesopotamia (Judg. 3:7–11).

■ *The territory given to Judah by Joshua corre-*
■ *sponded in large measure to the later South-*
■ *ern Kingdom of Judah which was ruled by*
■ *the Davidic line from Jerusalem.*

Caleb's Inheritance (15:13–19)

After receiving his inheritance at Hebron (14:1–15), Caleb proceeded to drive out the local Canaanites (Anakites) who lived there (15:13–14). His nephew Othniel captured Debir, a city south of Hebron on the road which drops into the Negev (15:15–17), and accepted Achsah, the daughter of Caleb, as his reward. Achsah asked for and received from her father the upper and lower springs of Debir as a dowry (15:18–19); even today these springs continue to provide a double blessing in an arid land.

■ *Caleb provides a good example of an Israel-*
■ *ite taking the initiative to conquer and settle*
■ *the land given to him by the Lord.*

The Cities of Judah (15:20–63)

The remainder of chapter 15 contains a list of the cities of Judah. This list divides into eleven distinct and contiguous geographical districts covering the Negev (15:21–32), the *shephelah* (15:33–36, 37–41, 42–44), the coastal plain (15:45–47), the hill country (15:48–51, 52–54, 55–57, 58–59, 60), and the wilderness bordering the Dead Sea (15:61–62). A twelfth district, covering the northern Judean hill country around Jerusalem and Bethlehem, is included in the Greek translation (Septuagint) of verse 59.

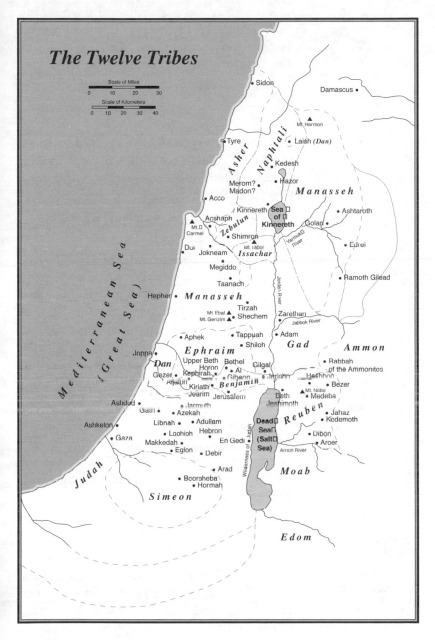

Taken from *Holman Bible Handbook,* (Nashville, Tenn.: Holman Bible Publishers, 1992), 204.

Many scholars believe that these groups, with the exception of the cities of the coastal plain in verses 45–47, were administrative districts of Judah during the time of the Israelite monarchy.

■ *The city list of Judah was included in the*
■ *book of Joshua to confirm that Joshua was*
■ *able to claim all of the land eventually settled*
■ *by Judah.*

THE ALLOTMENT TO THE TRIBES OF JOSEPH (16:1–17:18)

Ephraim and Manasseh, the sons of Joseph, received their inheritance because Joseph's father Jacob (Israel, Gen. 32:28) had counted them among his own sons (Gen. 48:1–22). The territory which the Joseph tribes were allotted, the central hill country of Canaan, became the heartland of the Northern Kingdom of Israel.

The Territory of Ephraim (16:1–10)

The tribe of Ephraim was granted the rugged hill country circumscribed by Bethel on the south, Jericho and the Jordan River on the east, the region of Shechem on the north and the Mediterranean Sea on the west. Like the heartland of Judah, the land of Ephraim was especially suited to vineyards and olive trees, the staple crops of ancient Israelite agriculture.

Within the territory of Ephraim lay Shiloh, the first religious center of ancient Israel (18:1; 1 Sam. 1:3), and Timnath Heres, the city which Joshua received for his own inheritance (19:49–50; cp. Judg. 2:9). Ephraim was unable to drive the Canaanites out of Gezer, a powerful Canaanite stronghold on the southwestern border of Ephraim guarding the main road to

In his blessing on the tribes of Joseph, Jacob anticipated Ephraim's favored inheritance in Canaan: "Joseph is a fruitful vine, a fruitful vine near a spring, whose branches climb over a wall" (Gen. 49:22). Moses added, "May the Lord bless his land with the precious dew from heaven above . . . with the best the sun brings forth and the finest the moon can yield; with the choicest gifts of the ancient mountains and the fruitfulness of the everlasting hills . . . let these rest on the head of Joseph" (Deut. 33:13–16).

Jerusalem from the west (16:10; cp. 10:33; Judg. 1:29; 1 Kings 9:16).

■ *The Ephraimites were largely successful in*
■ *settling their allotted territory, a rugged yet*
■ *fertile area which, together with the allot-*
■ *ment of Manasseh, formed the heartland of*
■ *the Northern Kingdom of Israel.*

The Territory of Manasseh (17:1–13)

The tribal inheritance of Manasseh was split between those members of this tribe who had remained east of the Jordan River (17:1–6; cp. 13:1–32) and those who settled north of the tribe of Ephraim (17:7–11). The agricultural possibilities of Manasseh were even more favorable than in Ephraim because the Manassite hills west of the Jordan River were not as rugged, and the valleys were more broad and inviting than the hill country of Ephraim. Eventually the three capital cities of the Northern Kingdom of Israel, Shechem (1 Kings 12:25), Tirzah (1 Kings 16:23) and Samaria (1 Kings 16:24), were located in the tribal territory of Manasseh.

Manasseh was also given land inhabited by several powerful Canaanite city-states: the broad Jezreel Valley (Plain of Esdraelon) with the cities of Megiddo, Taanach, and Ibleam; the city of Beth-Shean to the east; and the coastal plain in the vicinity of Dor (17:12). Neither Manasseh nor the later Israelite kings could totally defeat the Canaanites who lived there (17:13; cp. Judg. 1:27–28; 1 Kings 9:15).

■ *Like Ephraim, Manasseh was given a good*
■ *and fertile land. Neither tribe, however, was*
■ *able to totally subdue the Canaanites living*
■ *in their midst.*

The Initiative of the Joseph Tribes (17:14–18)

The account of the tribal allotment to Judah began with a story of a bold initiative undertaken by an old man to claim a difficult parcel of land which had been given to him (14:1–15). In stark contrast, the account of the tribal allotments to Ephraim and Manasseh ends with their men complaining to Joshua that they had not been given enough land in which to live comfortably (17:14). Joshua responded that their inheritance was sufficient if they would take the initiative to clear the forests and drive out the Canaanites (17:15–18).

Recent archaeological work in the hill country of Canaan shows that Israelite settlement developed first in the areas apportioned to the Joseph tribes and only later spread to an appreciable extent into Judah. This is consistent in broad outline with the book of Joshua, which locates early Israelite settlement centers at Shiloh (18:1; 21:2) and Shechem (8:30–35; 24:1–28), cities given to Ephraim and Manasseh, and speaks of an expansion of settlement from the central hill country outward (17:14–18).

The contrast is evident, and again is reflected in the later history of ancient Israel. Throughout the period of the monarchy, the Southern Kingdom of Judah, although smaller in population and given a land less fertile than the Northern Kingdom of Israel, remained more faithful to God and so ended up having the favored position—where it really counts—in the long run.

■ *Over time, the tribes of Ephraim and*
■ *Manasseh expanded their holdings to fill*
■ *their allotted tribal areas. While their work*
■ *was good, that of Judah was better, reflecting*
■ *a greater faith commitment to God.*

THE ALLOTMENT TO THE SEVEN REMAINING TRIBES (18:1–19:51)

The remaining seven tribes received their inheritance after the settlement process was already underway and the tent of meeting (i.e., the tabernacle) had been erected in Shiloh (18:1–7). Under Joshua's initiative, the land that remained to be apportioned was divided into seven relatively equal units (18:8–9). Joshua then cast lots to determine the specific inheritance of each tribe (18:10). Because they were inheritors of the priesthood, the tribe of Levi was to receive special treatment later (21:1–45; cp. 13:14, 33).

The first lot fell to Benjamin (18:11–28). Benjamin received a narrow band of land between Judah and Ephraim. Their inheritance included the path of Joshua's initial penetration into Canaan: Jericho, the region around Ai, the plateau on which Gibeon was located, and the route heading west down which he had chased the coalition of southern kings after the battle at Gibeon.

The tribe of Simeon received as their land a portion of the territory which had been given to Judah but which Judah was unable to settle (19:1–9). This land was in the Negev, the arid southern extremity of Judah's inheritance. Simeon appears to have been absorbed by the more dominant tribe of Judah during the early Israelite monarchy.

To Zebulun was given a portion of Galilee midway between the Mediterranean Sea and the Sea of Galilee (19:10–16). Their land included broad, fertile valleys set between high hills. Nazareth, Jesus' boyhood home, was on one of these hills.

The strategic region of Benjamin, sandwiched as it was between the powerful tribes of Judah to the south and Ephraim/Manasseh to the north, was fought over continually during the first century of the divided kingdom (1 Kings 14:30; 15:16). The border between north and south was finally fixed at Mizpah (1 Kings 15:22), making somewhat more than half of Benjamin a holding of Judah, and the remainder a holding of Israel.

Solomon gave a significant portion of Asher's inheritance to the king of Tyre in exchange for Hiram's help in building the Jerusalem Temple (1 Kings 9:10–14).

In New Testament times, Jesus' ministry in Galilee was centered in the tribal inheritance of Naphtali.

Isaachar received a hilly region southwest of the Sea of Galilee which extended, apparently, into the Jezreel Valley (19:17–23). Archaeological research has suggested that the Israelites did not settle the hills of Issachar to any appreciable degree until some time after the period of the judges.

Asher was given a territory along the Mediterranean coast north of Mount Carmel which stretched to the hinterland of the Phoenician cities of Tyre and Sidon (19:24–31). Asher's hold on the Phoenician coast was tenuous throughout biblical history.

Naphtali's rather large inheritance in Galilee included the Sea of Galilee and regions west and north (19:32–39). This included Hazor and the international highway which passed through the city.

The seventh lot fell to the tribe of Dan. Dan received a narrow piece of land between Judah and Ephraim, extending from the hill country west of Benjamin to the Mediterranean Sea (19:40–48). This region includes the modern city of Tel Aviv and its suburbs. During the period of the judges, the tribe of Dan left its tribal inheritance and migrated to the far north, where they conquered and resettled the city of Laish, renaming it Dan (Judg. 18:1–31).

After seeing to it that all Israel had received their inherited land, Joshua took possession of his own inheritance which was given him in turn by Israel (19:49–51). Joshua spent the rest of his life in Timnath-serah, a small farming village tucked away in the rugged hill country of Ephraim.

- Each tribe of Israel received an inheritance
- in the Promised Land. Their life of wander-
- ing was finally over; their life of blessing
- could begin.

SPECIAL ALLOTMENTS (20:1–21:42)

Two matters yet remained to be determined: the designation of the cities of refuge in Canaan and a special inheritance for the Levites.

The Cities of Refuge (20:1–9)

According to the command of Moses (see Num. 35:9–15), Joshua designated three cities in Canaan as cities of refuge: Kedesh in northern Galilee, Shechem in the central hill country of Ephraim and Hebron (Kiriath-arba) in the southern hill country of Judah (20:1, 7). Moses had already designated three cities of refuge in Transjordan for the use of the tribes which settled there (20:8; cp. Deut. 4:41–43). Because these cities were about equally distant from one another, none was more than a day's journey from any point in the land.

The actual use of the six cities designated as places of refuge is not documented in Scripture. However, the Bible does record that refuge was also sought—and usually granted—at the altar in Jerusalem (1 Kings 1:50–53; 2:28–34; cp. Exod. 21:12–14).

The cities of refuge were places where a person who committed manslaughter could flee and wait until his case could be fairly judged (20:2–6, 9; cp. Num. 35:9–34; Deut. 19:4–21). This important provision in the Mosaic Law, grounded in the sanctity of the individual, was aimed at curtailing blood revenge.

- By designating cities of refuge, Joshua sought
- to instill in Israel the necessary structures to
- foster a just and righteous society.

The Levitical Cities (21:1–42)

The members of the tribe of Levi did not receive a single, contiguous territory like the other tribes, because "the offerings made by fire to the Lord, the God of Israel, are their inheritance" (13:14; cp. 13:33; Deut. 18:1–2). The tribe of Levi had been set aside by God to be priests for Israel (Exod. 32:25–29). They were to serve as intermediaries before God and hence their inheritance was God Himself rather than land.

According to a provision granted by Moses (Num. 35:1–8), Joshua designated 48 cities and their surrounding pasturelands—four in each of the twelve tribal inheritances—as special Levitical cities (21:1–42). In this way, the Levites would have a place to call home, and at the same time be evenly distributed among the tribes to serve Israel more effectively.

Because Ephraim and Manasseh, the two tribes of Joseph's sons, each received a separate land inheritance and the Levites did not, the total number of tribal inheritances remained at twelve, the number of Jacob's sons.

Of the three primary institutions of leadership in ancient Israel (king, priest, and prophet), the priesthood was the most enduring. This was in no small measure due to the priests' having lived among the general populace of ancient Israel. The priesthood became the primary focus of Jewish authority and life in the intertestamental period and remained so until A.D. 70, when the Temple, the focal point of their work, was destroyed by the Romans. The priests' role as teachers of the law was eventually replaced by the Pharisees and synagogue rabbis of Judaism.

■ *The priests received homes throughout the*
■ *land in order to serve the ongoing religious*
■ *and social needs of ancient Israel more effec-*
■ *tively.*

A SUMMARY OF THE ALLOTMENT OF CANAAN (21:43–45)

The author of the book of Joshua ended his account of the allotment of Canaan with a statement that the promises of land which God had made to Israel had been "fulfilled" (21:45; cp. Gen. 12:1; 13:14–15; 15:12–21; 26:3; 28:13;

35:12; Deut. 31:1–8, 23; Josh. 1:2). With their land, "the Lord gave [Israel] rest on every side" so that "not one of their enemies withstood them" (21:44). Israel was thus given every opportunity to enjoy their new homeland.

This summary presents an optimistic picture of Israel's future. The entire land had been allotted and hence "claimed" by Joshua for Israel. While not all of the Canaanites had been defeated (see 13:1–7), Israel's hold on the land was assured as long as they remained faithful to God's covenant (see Deut. 30:15–20; Josh. 1:3–9).

■ *In bringing Israel into their land and allow-*
■ *ing them to settle down there, God had*
■ *shown that He was faithful to His covenant.*
■ *Now it was Israel's turn to live faithfully*
■ *before God.*

QUESTIONS TO GUIDE YOUR STUDY

1. Compare the blessings of Jacob (Gen. 49:1–27) and Moses (Deut. 33:1–29) with the description of the land allotted to each of the tribes by Joshua. How does one complement the other? What is the overall picture gained?

2. Compare and contrast the attitude of Caleb with that of the other tribes. Is anything special being said about the tribe of Judah through the story of Caleb?

3. How did Joshua give the Levites opportunity to serve Israel?

COVENANT MATTERS (22:1–24:33)

Thematically, the book of Joshua ends the way it began—with attention focused on God's covenant with Israel. Joshua had been encouraged by God to remain faithful to his calling (1:2–6), but in the end he had serious doubts about his peoples' commitment to do the same.

THE DEPARTURE OF THE TRANSJORDAN TRIBES (22:1–34)

The departure of the tribes of Reuben and Gad and the half-tribe of Manasseh to Transjordan was accompanied by mistrust and misunderstanding on the part of the rest of Israel. Scarcely had Israel begun to settle their land when seeds of unrest were sown.

The Return Home (22:1–9)

With the conquest and allotment of Canaan essentially complete, Joshua sent the tribes which had received their inheritance east of the Jordan River back to their homes. As they had faithfully helped their fellow Israelites conquer Canaan, so they now must continue to faithfully love, serve, and follow God in all His ways (22:1–6).

The Transjordan tribes returned home loaded with spoil from the conquest of Canaan (22:7–9). Their enrichment at the expense of the Canaanites was further indication that God's blessing had been poured out on His chosen people in tangible ways (see Gen. 20:14–16; Exod. 12:35–36; Num. 31:25–54; Mal. 3:10).

Joshua's exhortation to the Transjordan tribes echoed Moses' instruction in Deuteronomy 6:5: "Love the Lord your God with all your heart and with all your soul and with all your might." On more than one occasion, Jesus quoted this command when asked what was the heart of the law (Matt. 22:34–40; Mark 12:28–34; Luke 10:25–28).

■ *The Transjordan tribes returned home with*
■ *Joshua's blessing, their pockets full and their*
■ *hearts satisfied with a job well done.*

The Dispute Over an Altar (22:10–34)

Just before returning home, the tribes of Reuben and Gad and the half-tribe of Manasseh built a large altar, patterned after that at Shiloh, on the Canaan side of the Jordan River (22:10–11). When the other tribes heard of it, they immediately threatened war, reasoning that the Transjordan tribes were abandoning God and His covenant by erecting an unsanctioned altar to rival the one at Shiloh (22:12–20). It was assumed that this altar violated God's command in Deuteronomy that Israel have a single valid sanctuary (Deut. 12:1–14).

A delegation was sent to confront the offending tribes. This delegation was told that the altar was to serve only as a memorial to future generations who might wonder if the Transjordan tribes, separated as they were from the tribes in Canaan, were really part of God's chosen people (22:21–29, 34). This answer satisfied both the delegation and Israel (22:30–33).

When offended by others, most of us quickly become provoked. Jesus gave instructions that conflict should be handled first by those immediately involved in the trouble (Matt. 18:15–20). By dealing with conflict at its source, it is possible to avoid escalation which so often brings ruin to the cause of Christ.

■ *The Israelites almost came to civil war over*
■ *a misunderstanding that involved God's cov-*
■ *enant. While the resolution was peaceful, it*
■ *foreshadowed other more serious intratribal*
■ *conflicts in the years ahead.*

JOSHUA'S FAREWELL ADDRESS (23:1–16)

Joshua had grown old, and it was time for him to say good-bye to his people (23:1). He called Israel together and preached a short sermon modeled after Moses' farewell speech in the book of Deuteronomy (see Deut. 31:1–21).

Israel had been successful so far because God was fighting for them (23:3; cp. 5:13–15; 10:10; 11:8; Deut. 31:3–8). He would continue to fulfill His promises to Israel (23:4–5; cp. with Deut. 31:7), but Israel must respond by remaining firm in their resolve to keep God's laws (23:6; see also Deut. 31:9–13).

The Hebrew verb "to cling to" is used primarily to designate a very close physical proximity between two objects (see Job 19:20; Jer. 13:11; Lam. 4:4). By extension, it also indicates the affection and loyalty which results when two people share an intimate tie with one another (for example, Adam and Eve, Gen. 2:24, and Ruth and Naomi, Ruth 1:14).

The primary danger which Israel faced in Canaan was idolatry—pursuing gods other than the God who had delivered and entered into covenant with them. Israel was to "cling to" the Lord their God (23:7–11; cp. Deut. 10:20; 11:22). If they chose instead to "cling to" the ways of the nations around them, the nations would again gain the upper hand, "and you will quickly perish from the good land he has given you" (23:12–13, 16). Joshua warned that if God was able to keep His promises to bring good things to Israel—and throughout the lifetime of Joshua he had proven that he could—then He was also able to keep His promise to take away Israel's blessings if He thought it necessary (24:14–16).

- *The choice was simple—at least it was sim-*
- *ply said. If Israel remained faithful, they*
- *would enjoy the blessings which God had in*
- *store for them in their own land. If not, God*
- *would take away their inheritance.*

COVENANT RENEWAL AT SHECHEM (24:1–28)

Years before, Israel had renewed the covenant at Shechem by reciting the blessings and curses which would befall them, depending on their faithfulness to its terms (8:30–35). Now Joshua again called the people before God at Shechem for a final time of covenant renewal (24:1).

Joshua first reviewed Israel's history, beginning with God's call of Abraham and ending with the recently completed conquest of Canaan (24:2–12). The Land of Promise was a gift, and Israel was not to forget it (24:13).

God's mighty acts of deliverance on behalf of Israel formed the basis of Joshua's plea for covenant obedience. Each Israelite was to make a deliberate choice—either for God or against Him (24:14–15). The former choice would allow Israel to participate in God's plan for the world; the latter would take them back to Mesopotamia, the region from which Abraham had come.

"Your choice [for God] must be a deliberate determination—it is not something into which you will automatically drift."
Oswald Chambers, *My Utmost for His Highest*, July 8.

The people agreed to serve God exclusively (24:16–18), but Joshua, like Moses before him, knew better (24:19–20; cp. Deut. 31:14–22). Nevertheless, Joshua made a covenant with Israel at Shechem by ratifying their promise to remain faithful to God (24:21–25). Joshua recorded the covenant in the book of the law, erected a large stone as a permanent witness to his people's pledge, and sent Israel home, "each to his own inheritance" (24:26–28).

- God's people reaffirmed the covenant in a
- solemn ceremony at Shechem. After this,
- there was nothing left unsaid or
- undone—Israel, fully responsible for their
- own behavior, left to begin a new life in their
- new homeland.

THE PASSING OF A GENERATION (24:29–33)

The book of Joshua ends with three important death notices. Joshua, who could be called "servant of the Lord" after a lifetime of faithful service (24:29; cp. 1:1), died and was buried in his inheritance in Timnath Serah (24:29–31). The bones of Joseph, brought by Israel out of Egypt, were buried in his ancestral home in Shechem (24:32). Finally, Eleazar, the high priest and son of Aaron, died and was buried in his inheritance in the town of Gibeah (24:33). Each of these cities, plus Shiloh, was in the hill country of Ephraim (cp. 20:7)—testimony that the focal point of Israel's initial settlement was the central hill country of Canaan.

- With the death of Joshua, a generation of
- faithful leadership had passed from the scene
- in Israel. Joshua, Moses' successor, had
- served God well. But who would follow him?

QUESTIONS TO GUIDE YOUR STUDY

1. What lessons does the incident of the altar in Joshua 22 teach for interpersonal conflict and reconciliation?

2. How does the emphasis on covenant in chapters 1, 8–9 and 24 of Joshua serve to tie the book together? What issues are emphasized? What themes are repeated?

3. Has your analysis of Joshua's leadership abilities changed as you encountered him in the biblical text? Given the complexities of today's world, should we hold Joshua up as a realistic model of effective leadership?

JUDGES, INTRODUCTION

The book of Judges receives its title from the military and civil leaders who delivered Israel from foreign oppressors during the centuries between the conquest of Canaan under Joshua and the rise of the kingship with Saul and David. The title of the book in Hebrew, the language in which it was written, is *Shophtim*, which means "Judges."

The judges of the book of Judges were not civil magistrates as the word usually indicates today. Rather, they were Spirit-empowered deliverers (3:9–10) who brought justice to the people of Israel when they were oppressed by foreign powers. Some of these judges appear to have enjoyed a long-standing role of leadership in ancient Israel, while others were called by God only to lead a specific military campaign. To avoid confusion, the NIV has often translated "led" rather than "judged" to describe the activity of these judges (see 4:4; 10:2–3; 12:8, 11, 13; 15:20; 16:31).

AUTHOR, AUDIENCE, AND DATE OF WRITING

Like Joshua, the book of Judges is anonymous. Early Jewish and Christian tradition held that the author of Judges was the prophet Samuel, who lived at the end of the period of the judges. However, it is highly unlikely that this was the case. Clues within the book itself suggest that Judges was written at least during the time of the Israelite monarchy (17:6; 18:1; 19:1; 21:25) if not later (18:30).

There is a general scholarly consensus that the author of Judges used existing oral or written sources in compiling his book. For instance, based on vocabulary and style, the Song of Deborah (5:1–31) appears to be one of the oldest Israelite compositions. In addition, the episodes of the judges give the appearance of having been independent stories at one time. However, it is impossible to arrive at any conclusions regarding the process by which Judges was written other than to be sure that its composition was inspired and directed by God (2 Tim. 3:16).

Along with Joshua, 1 and 2 Samuel, and 1 and 2 Kings, the book of Judges is considered to be both one of the Former Prophets and part of the Deuteronomic History. These terms are explained in the introductory material to the book of Joshua, and what is said there applies for the book of Judges as well.

HISTORICAL CONTEXT OF THE EVENTS RECORDED IN JUDGES

Specific dating formulae are given throughout the book of Judges regarding the length of time that Israel was oppressed, as well as the number of years the land had "rest" from war prior to its next period of oppression. Often these figures are given in round numbers (twenty, forty, or eighty years), and it is almost certain that together they should not be taken to indicate a single, unbroken chain of years. Because only a few of the tribes were involved with each of the oppressions, it is likely that the activities of the judges overlapped.

For these reasons, it is difficult if not impossible to provide exact dates for events of the book of Judges based on the biblical evidence alone. Evidence from archaeology can help, but because archaeological work is by nature incomplete and open to interpretation, it can seldom provide definitive answers. Specific questions of dating in Judges remain open.

During the time of the judges, other peoples which surrounded Israel—such as the Philistines on the coastal plain to the southwest, the Edomites, Moabites and Ammonites in Transjordan to the east, and various Phoenician peoples along the coast to the northwest—were developing the social and political structures which would lead to the establishment of kingship in

The events recorded in Judges took place from the end of the period which archaeologists and historians call the Late Bronze Age (primarily the twelfth century B.C.) to the end of Iron Age I (1200–1000 B.C.). These centuries saw a sharp increase in population in the rugged hill country which lies between Jerusalem and the Jezreel Valley (plain of Esdraelon), the area of Canaan which Joshua had apportioned to the tribes of Ephraim and Manasseh. Most Israelites lived in simple farming villages or herded mixed flocks of sheep and goats on the arid slopes that dropped eastward toward the Jordan Valley. The twelve Israelite tribes seem to have been loosely confederated around the central religious site of Shiloh, the major center in the hill country of Ephraim where the tabernacle and ark of the covenant were located.

their own lands. As these emergent nations looked outward, it was natural that their priorities would clash at times with those of Israel.

PURPOSE

The covenant which God had established with Israel at Mount Sinai (Exod. 19:5–20:20) demanded Israel's exclusive obedience to God. The gods of Canaan and those of the nations surrounding Israel were to have no place in Israelite life or thought. However, the longer the Israelites lived among the Canaanites, the more susceptible they became to Canaanite religious practices. Various problems of religious and moral syncretism plagued Israel throughout the centuries between the conquest of Canaan under Joshua and their exile to Babylon by Nebuchadnezzar in 586 B.C.

Looking back at the history of God's people, the authors of the books of the Deuteronomic History sought to instruct and warn Israel about the dangers of ignoring the Lord in the circumstances of their daily lives. Judges connects the economic and political fortunes of Israel between the time of the conquest and the rise of the kingship with the spiritual state of its people.

When God's people forgot Him and "did evil in the eyes of the Lord" (2:11; 3:7, 12; 4:1; 6:1; 10:6; 13:1), God allowed foreign enemies to oppress Israel. When Israel turned back to God, God raised up deliverers (judges) to restore them. While the judges were largely successful in subduing Israel's foreign enemies, Israel's ongoing cycle of rebellion against God finally led to civil war (20:1–48). The author of Judges reminded his readers that such problems occurred because "in those days Israel had no king; everyone did as he saw fit" (17:6; 18:1; 19:1; 21:25).

When read as a part of the larger Deuteronomic History, the book of Judges warned the Israelites that if their apostasy continued during the period of the monarchy (when there *was* a king in Israel who could lead the people to do what was right in God's eyes—1 Kings 15:5), a period of foreign oppression would occur which would far surpass the troubles of the days of the judges. That oppression, clearly foreseen by the biblical prophets, was the Babylonian Exile (2 Kings 24:1–25:26; Hab. 1:5–17).

The purpose of the book of Judges, then, was to teach Israel that the reasons why they were not enjoying the covenant blessings now that they lived in their own land (cp. Deut. 28:1–14) was that they were not keeping the terms of the covenant which God had demanded (2:11–23). The problems which faced Israel as a nation lay with the response of each individual to God.

STRUCTURE AND CONTENT

The book of Judges divides into three parts based on content:

1. An introduction that sets the tone for the book in explaining why some of the land of Canaan had not been conquered by Israel (1:1–2:5);
2. Stories about the lives of the individual judges (2:6–16:31); and
3. Stories detailing the religious apostasy of Israel (17:1–21:25).

The stories of the judges concentrate on Israel's foreign affairs, while those recorded in chapters 17–21 relate problems which tore Israel apart from within.

The book of Judges is best known for the stories of Deborah, Gideon, and Samson. These three leaders were part of a recurring cycle of oppression and deliverance which was used by the writer of Judges to depict the uneasy condition of ancient Israel following the death of Joshua and preceding the rise of the kingship under Saul and David. The four stages of this cycle are described in Judges 2:11–19, and illustrated in chapters 3–16:

1. *Rebellion.* "Then the Israelites did evil in the eyes of the Lord" (2:11–13).
2. *Retribution.* "In his anger against Israel the LORD handed them over to raiders who plundered them. He sold them to their enemies all around" (2:14–15).
3. *Repentance.* "The Lord had compassion on them as they groaned" (2:18).
4. *Restoration.* "Then the Lord raised up judges who delivered them from those who plundered them" (2:16–18), so that "the land had rest" for a certain number of years (3:11, 30).

Invariably, after the judge who delivered Israel had died, the people would begin the cycle anew by again rebelling against God. The cycle spiraled downward with the end result that Israel—and its leaders—became unable to cope with the many problems that plagued them from without and within.

The judges whose activities included military battles (Othniel, Ehud, Shamgar, Deborah, Gideon, Jephthah, and Samson) are often called "major judges." This is to distinguish them from the five lesser-known judges (Tola, Jair, Ibzan, Elon, and Abdon) whose leadership role appears to have been more institutional and less heroic. To highlight this difference, these five men are often called "minor judges." The exploits of Abimelech, the strong-willed son of Gideon, are detailed in Judges 9, even though he was not called by God and therefore was not properly a judge. The era of the judges actually ended with Eli, Samuel, and the sons of Samuel; men whose ministry is recorded in 1 Samuel 1:1–8:3.

The book of Ruth, appearing between Judges and 1 Samuel in English translations of the Old Testament, records a story of hope and faith which took place during the turbulent days of the judges. The tender story of Ruth is a welcome reminder that, even when chaos reigns on every side of God's people, He always preserves a faithful remnant that is able to receive His blessings.

The last section of Judges (chapters 17–21) is called an appendix by some, but it is actually an integral part of the book. It relates two incidents which portray graphically the result of the downward spiral presented in chapters 3–16. The stories of the migration of the tribe of Dan and the Israelite civil war show that even though Israel by and large was able to subdue its foreign enemies, they were increasingly unable to create a workable society at home.

LITERARY STYLE

Like the book of Joshua, Judges is classified as a narrative. Judges tells an overall, unified story composed of a number of shorter episodes. Each of the episodes which make up the whole "hangs together" by itself with a unique cast of characters, a different geographical setting and a clear introduction, plot, and conclusion. The writer of Judges was a masterful narrator who wove together in an intricate fashion sophisticated literary elements such as word play, metaphor, irony, allusion, paradox, and the patterned repetition of words, phrases, themes, and ideas. Judges deserves to be read slowly, carefully, and often.

The stories of Judges are of varying character and length. Some, such as those of Gideon (chaps. 6–8), Samson (chaps. 13–16) and the civil war (chaps. 19–21), are similar to a modern short story. Others, such as the episodes of Othniel (3:7–11) and Shamgar (3:31), are closer to an anecdote. The activities of the five so-called "minor" judges are recorded as if taken from an official annal or archive (10:1–5; 12:8–15). The Song of Deborah (5:1–31), a brilliant composition, is one of the oldest Hebrew poems known. These differing literary units are all bound together by introductory comments in chapters 2 and 3 which explain the downward cycle of apostasy into which Israel was repeatedly drawn.

Judges, like Joshua, is also historical. Its stories are a straightforward, plain (although artistic) telling of what happened to ancient Israel. Judges gives every indication that its author intended his book to be read realistically, as a true account (albeit from God's point of view) of a specific period of Israel's past.

THEOLOGY

Among the biblical truths taught in the book of Judges are:

- people naturally tend to turn away from God (2:10–19; 3:7);
- sin has negative consequences (2:20–23; 3:5–8);
- human self-will, without thought of God's will, is folly (17:6; 21:25);
- people are unable to solve their own problems without the guidance and help of God (4:1–3; 6:6; 10:13–14);
- each generation needs to pass the knowledge of God's ways on to the next generation (2:10);
- everyone, especially God's people, needs solid, righteous leadership (2:6–10; 21:25);
- God's sovereign purposes for the nations and for His people will not be thwarted (2:1); and
- People are empowered when they are filled with God's Spirit (3:10; 6:16, 34; 13:25).

Theologically, the book of Judges shows the need for a Savior. Without divine intervention, people are hopelessly lost. The decisions of individuals affect other people and society at large, all of which stand in need of God's redemption.

The book of Joshua portrays the faithfulness of Israel in conquering their land, and the blessings from God which resulted from being faithful (Josh 11:23). Judges presents an opposite picture: Israel, especially when lacking effective leadership, was naturally unfaithful to God (2:6–10; 21:25). God, however, remained faithful to His covenant even though His people did not. He also showed Himself to be the true leader and deliverer of His chosen people and the sovereign judge of the nations which stand outside of His covenant.

THE MEANING OF JUDGES FOR TODAY

By itself, the book of Judges is gloomy. Left to their own devices, people invariably choose what is less than best—and, sometimes, what is downright bad—for themselves. In Genesis, God told Adam and Eve that they were not to eat of the tree of life and the tree of the knowledge of good and evil (Gen. 2:16–17; 3:1–7). This was not because these trees had magical qualities but because they signaled the right which God alone possesses to grant life and determine what is good and what is not good for people: His special creation. By ignoring God during the days of the judges, the Israelites continued to usurp God's right to determine what is good for people. Judges, more than any other book in the early portion of the Old Testament, shows the outworking of the Fall recorded in Genesis (see Gen. 3).

The good news is that, for the Israelites, God provided a means of escape. By believing in God and following His word that was revealed through Moses, the Israelites could learn how to live wisely in their Promised Land. By carefully arranging their lives to follow God's will and by diligently teaching His word and ways to their children (cp. Deut. 4:9; 6:4–8), the Israelites had the opportunity to live blessed lives in a blessed land.

All people—believers and unbelievers alike—have the opportunity to see reflections of themselves in the characters who move along the pages of Judges. Like Samson, our desires too often take control. Like Jophthah, we ask, "What's in it for me?" Like Barak, we often want to stand up for God, but first need the support of others to do so. Sometimes, like Gideon, we feel as though we need a personal message from God before we do what we really know needs to be done. Sometimes, like Ehud or Deborah, we follow God willingly. The good news is that with Jesus, Christians do not have to fall back on their own devices when facing the many challenges of life. Through His Spirit and His revealed Word, God provides the strength we need for each day.

The book of Judges is a sad sequel to the book of Joshua. The optimism of Joshua's day quickly gave way to a morass of foreign oppression and tribal infighting that was permeated by a loss of spiritual direction. By forsaking the instruction and warnings of Moses and Joshua for the ways of the nations, Israel began to lose its distinctiveness as the people of God.

CONQUEST SUCCESSES (1:1–26)

The opening verses of Judges focus on a few successful attempts to conquer cities in and around Judah. Some of these conquests, but evidently not all, took place after the death of Joshua (Judg. 1:1). Although the information given is rather sketchy, the overall thrust is that the Israelites were able to continue the work of Joshua within the territory of Judah.

With the help of their allied tribe Simeon, the men of Judah conquered Bezek and its king, Adoni-Bezek ("the lord of Bezek"; 1:1–7). By mutilating Adoni-Bezek and forcing him to eat like a dog under the table (cp. Matt. 15:27), Israel showed him the same inhumane treatment which he had forced on others.

The conquest of Jerusalem and Debir in Judges 1:8–15 evidently repeats those conquests recorded in Joshua 10:3, 16–27; 12:10; 15:13–19, only from a different perspective. By mentioning these conquests at the beginning of Judges, the author sought to tie his book thematically to Joshua, yet provide a significant shift in emphasis. In Joshua, the tribe of Ephraim was in the forefront; in Judges, it was Judah that conquered and settled their land while the other tribes had difficulty doing the same (cp. 1:21; 27–36). This theological emphasis on Judah has led some interpreters to conclude that the book was written from the point of view of the Southern Kingdom of Judah, the tribe from which the Davidic monarchy would spring.

Yet even Judah was not altogether successful. They, together with the Kenites (1:16), conquered other areas of their tribal inheritance (for example, the southern Negev—1:16–17; the coastal plain—1:18; and the hill country—1:19–20), but they could not always hold their gains (1:19, 21).

Finally, Judges notes that the Joseph tribes, Ephraim and Manasseh, were successful in conquering Bethel (1:22–26), the city which eventually became the southern border point and primary religious center of the Northern Kingdom of Israel (1 Kings 12:29–33).

■ *The conquest of Canaan continued at an*
■ *erratic pace after the death of Joshua. The*
■ *few successes mentioned gave prominence to*
■ *the tribe of Judah.*

CONQUEST FAILURES (1:27–2:5)

Conquest proved to be the exception rather than the rule in the generations following the death of Joshua. The rest of the first chapter of Judges is filled with notices of failure to conquer the land which had been allotted by Joshua to the various tribes of Israel (1:27–36). For the

After killing the men who had murdered Ishbosheth, son of Saul, David desecrated their bodies by cutting off their hands and feet (2 Sam. 4:12). Such postbattle mutilation was consistent with warfare practices in the ancient Near East. Maiming was also proscribed by the Mosaic Law as punishment for certain heinous crimes (Lev. 24:19–20; Deut. 25:11–12).

The word *angel* means "messenger." The angel of the Lord plays a prominent role in Judges, usually bringing special announcements from God or calling a judge to action (2:1, 4; 5:23; 6:11–22; 13:3–21). Most consider the angel of the Lord to have been a being who carried the presence of God in a way that superseded that of ordinary angels. Some hold that the angel of the Lord can only be explained as a pre-incarnate appearance of Christ.

most part, the cities not conquered were located on the coastal plain or in large inland valleys, traditional strongholds of Canaanite culture (note especially 1:34). These cities were not subdued until the time of David. Each notice includes the remark that the Canaanites dwelt among the Israelites, an indication of the cultural and religious syncretism which characterized so much of later Israelite history.

The angel of the Lord was sent to explain why Israel had failed to conquer the entire land (2:1–5). The angel's announcement put in capsule form the repeated warnings of Moses (see Exod. 23:32–33; Num. 33:55; Deut. 7:16; 31:20) and Joshua (Josh. 23:13) that if Israel failed to keep the terms of God's covenant, they would have to share their land with the nations whom they should have driven out. True to these warnings, the nation of Canaan would prove to be a snare to Israel throughout their history, pulling the people away from God.

Israel realized their plight and wept, naming the place where the angel appeared to them "Bochim," or "weepers." It is unclear from the immediate context whether the people wept out of sincere repentance or because they were resigned to their fate. The rest of the book suggests that their contrition, however well meaning at the time, did not run deep.

■ *The tone of Judges is set by the ominous*
■ *announcement of the angel of the Lord. The*
■ *unfaithfulness of God's people has ongoing*
■ *consequences which result in their missing*
■ *out on God's blessings.*

QUESTIONS TO GUIDE YOUR STUDY

1. How do the opening verses of Judges differ in tenor from the opening verses of Joshua? What can you expect to read in Judges as a result?
2. Why did the writer of Judges repeat information about the conquest of Canaan that was already given in the book of Joshua?
3. Why do you think that the angel of the Lord appeared to Israel at this time in their history?

The heart of the book of Judges contains stories of the judges who delivered Israel from foreign oppression. While each was effective in delivering Israel, taken together they show a marked digression in moral character and the ability to remain faithful to the stipulations of God's covenant.

ISRAEL'S SPIRITUAL APOSTASY (2:6–3:6)

The writer of Judges introduced his stories of the individual judges by mentioning the death of Joshua, the great event which marked the end of Israel's formative years and the beginning of life in the Promised Land (2:6–10; cp. Josh. 24:29–30). While Joshua was alive, the people had served God (2:7), but after he was gone, a generation arose "who knew neither the Lord nor what he had done for Israel" (2:10). This phrase sets the stage for the statement which appears repeatedly at the end of the book of Judges: "In those days Israel had no king, and everyone did as he saw fit" (17:6; 18:1; 19:1; 21:25).

Without righteous leadership, God's people fell away from Him. Israel turned—quite naturally, as the doctrine of sin makes clear (Rom. 7:13–20)—to the ways of the world around them (2:11–13). The writer of Judges described the cycle of sin into which Israel fell: Israel abandoned God and so suffered under foreign oppression; Israel cried out to God and He sent judges to deliver them; whenever the judge

"No matter what we sow, the law of returns applies. Good or evil, love or hate, justice or tyranny, grapes or thorns, a gracious compliment or a peevish complaint—whatever we invest, we tend to get it back with interest. Lovers are loved; haters, hated. Forgivers usually get forgiven; those who live by the sword die by the sword. 'God is not mocked, for you reap whatever you sow.'" Cornelius Plantinga, Jr., *Not the Way It's Supposed to Be: A Breviary of Sin* (Grand Rapids, Eerdmans), p. 68.

died, Israel turned from God and the cycle began anew (2:14–19). God allowed the nations in and around Canaan to test Israel's commitment to Him, but they repeatedly failed the test (2:20–3:6).

- *People do as they please. God has provided*
- *guidance for His people, but the natural ten-*
- *dency is to ignore His ways for our own.*

THE EARLY JUDGES (3:7–8:35)

The period of the judges divides easily into two sections joined by the story of the abortive kingship of Abimelech, son of Gideon. The first section includes the judges Othniel, Ehud, Shamgar, Deborah, Barak, and Gideon—an unlikely mix of persons who provided effective leadership for Israel.

Othniel (3:7–11)

The first judge was Othniel, the son of Caleb's brother, Kenaz. Othniel was already known in Israel as the one who had conquered Debir and married Caleb's daughter as a reward (1:11–15; cp. Josh. 15:13–19). Empowered by the Spirit of the Lord, Othniel delivered Israel from Cushan-Rishathaim, king of Mesopotamia (3:8, 10).

The story of Othniel differs from the other judges in its universal scope. Unlike the other judges, Othniel did not face one of Israel's immediate neighbors but rather the "king of Mesopotamia," a generic title pointing to the mighty empires of the east which would so trouble Israel during the latter days of the monarchy. Furthermore, while the activity of the other judges was limited to one or at most

The name *Cushan-rishathaim* means "the doubly wicked one from Cush." The land of Cush in the Bible is usually identified with Ethiopia (Isa. 18:1; Ezek. 29:10). On the basis of Genesis 2:13 and 10:8, however, it probably also refers to a region in Mesopotamia inhabited by the Kassites, a people from the Iranian highlands who dominated Mesopotamia in the period of the judges.

A period of time designated "forty years" was equal to one generation (3:11; cp. Num. 14:26–33). When the Bible states that the land had rest (i.e., peace) from war for forty years until the judge who had delivered Israel died, it probably means that for an entire generation—the adult lifetime of the judge—Israel remained free from foreign oppression.

several of the tribes, Othniel appears to have delivered all Israel. The paradigm of an effective judge was thus set: total deliverance from the most powerful of enemies. No other judge met this standard.

■ *Othniel provided effective leadership for the*
■ *first generation of post-Joshua Israelites. His*
■ *ties to Joshua through Caleb served him well,*
■ *but he did not inherit Joshua's role as perma-*
■ *nent leader over all Israel.*

Ehud and Shamgar (3:12–31)

The story of Ehud is entertaining and full of intrigue. Eglon, king of Moab, had taken possession of Jericho, the City of Palms (3:13; cp. Deut. 34:3), thereby controlling the Israelite religious center of Gilgal and the crucial eastern highways into and out of the central hill country. In effect, Eglon was retracing Joshua's footsteps in order to claim Israel's Promised Land for Moab.

Because the tribe of Benjamin was most effected by Eglon's intrusion, God raised its local hero, Ehud, to action (3:15). Concealing a short sword under his robe, Ehud unsuspectingly used his left hand to assassinate Eglon during an interview in his private chamber (3:15–25). Upon escaping, Ehud rallied the men of Ephraim to defeat the now leaderless Moabites and deliver Israel (3:26–30).

A goad was a long, straight stick of oak or other strong wood tipped with a sharpened iron point (1 Sam. 13:21) and used to prod oxen or cattle when plowing (cp. Eccl. 12:11; Acts 26:14). Shamgar used an ox goad as a weapon much like a javelin or spear.

Appended to the story of Ehud is a note that Shamgar delivered Israel by killing six hundred Philistines with an ox goad (3:31). He lived during the time that Israel was oppressed by Jabin, king of Hazor (5:6).

■ *Ehud and Shamgar were effective judges of*
■ *Israel. Their willingness to be used by God*
■ *provided Israel the means by which to live in*
■ *peace for two generations. Slowly, however,*
■ *the cycle of sin and punishment began to*
■ *tighten.*

Deborah and Barak (4:1–5:31)

The story of Israel's deliverance under Deborah
and Barak is told twice, once as a narrative and
once as a poetic song. These two tellings complement each other and provide a unique look
at the way Israel remembered its past.

The Call of Barak (4:1–10)

After Ehud died, Israel's unfaithfulness so weakened the tribes that they fell under the control of
Jabin, "king of Canaan, who reigned in Hazor"
(4:1–2). Joshua had defeated a "Jabin king of
Hazor" who led a large coalition of Canaanite
kings against him during the conquest of
Canaan (Josh. 11:1–14). "Jabin" was probably
either a throne name of the kings of Hazor or
simply a popular name liked by the Hazor royal
family. Jabin's formidable army, far greater in
weaponry than anything that could be mustered
by Israel, was led by his able general, Sisera
(4:2–3).

Deborah was a popular prophetess who minis-
tered to Israel between Ramah and Bethel, the
same place where the prophet Samuel would
minister to a later generation (4:4–5; cp. 1 Sam.
7:15–17). God used her to call Barak—who was
from Kedesh in Naphtali and no doubt witnessed the oppression of Jabin firsthand—to
lead Israel in battle (4:6–7). Barak refused to

Although Hazor, the
largest city in Canaan,
was located north of
the Sea of Galilee, the
setting of the battle of
Deborah and Barak
was the Jezreel
Valley. The most
prominent
topographical feature
in the Jezreel Valley is
Mount Tabor,
standing like a
sentinel in its
northeastern corner
and guarding the
doorway to Hazor
from the south (4:6).
The Jezreel Valley is
drained to the west by
the Kishon River (4:7).
The location of
Harosheth Hagoyim
(4:2) is uncertain, but
it may be in the vicinity
of Megiddo. Kedesh
of Naphtali (4:10) is in
a remote area in the
hills just west of the
Sea of Galilee, a good
place to rally troops
for battle.

Deborah is one of several prominent women in the Bible who were effectively used by God in leadership roles. Among others are the prophetesses Miriam (Exod. 15:20) and Huldah (2 Kings 22:14–20), Queen Esther (Esther 2:15–9:32), Priscilla (Acts 18:18–26), and Phoebe (Rom. 16:1).

heed God's call unless the prophetess Deborah accompanied him; this was either a sign of cowardice or the way Barak chose to be sure that God would remain with him in battle (4:8–10). In either case, Barak's obedience was conditional, the first sign that the judges of Israel were beginning to waver.

- God began to deliver Israel through two
- unlikely candidates: Barak, a man of ques-
- tionable commitment, and Deborah, a
- woman. Eventually His choice would prove
- to be the right one, but in the meantime Jabin
- enjoyed free reign over Israel.

The Defeat of Jabin (4:11–24)

After mustering his troops, Barak chose to fight at Mount Tabor (4:12). Sisera arranged his chariots on the plain below the mountain, a location with clear tactical advantages (4:13). Barak attacked, and with God's help chased Sierra's army down the valley, where it was defeated (4:14–16). According to the poetic account of the battle recorded in Judges 5, Sierra's forces were swept away by the Kishon River (5:21). Evidently a thunderstorm bogged the chariot wheels and allowed Barak's foot soldiers to gain the upper hand.

The once-mighty Sisera, however, proved to be more of a coward than Barak. He fled the battle in the opposite direction and took refuge in the tent of Jael, an Israelite sympathizer (4:17; cp. v. 11). While Sisera may have intended to seize Jael as his spoil (cp. 5:28–30), she instead lulled him to sleep before deftly killing him (4:18–22).

With their back broken, Jabin's allied forces eventually succumbed to Israel (4:23–24).

- Israel was successful in defeating a superior
- foe, but only because God intervened on their
- behalf. God continued to show His power to
- Israel—but would Israel remain faithful to
- Him?

The Song of Deborah (5:1–31)

The Song of Deborah is a brilliant Israelite literary composition. It preserves in poetic form the victory of Deborah and Barak over Sisera and his forces. Even a cursory reading reveals the song's deep passion for God and His people; when God acts, nature itself responds by fighting for Israel (5:20–21).

This song is a good example of early Israelite poetry (but compare also Exod. 15:1–18; Deut. 32:1–43; 33:2–29; 2 Sam. 22:2–51). Its intricate use of parallelism—the defining characteristic of ancient Israelite poetry—and elaborate use of imagery are particularly striking.

The Song of Deborah begins, as does all early Israelite poetry, with praise to God, focusing on His revelation at Mount Sinai (5:2–5). It then tells the story of Deborah and Barak in a way that made it easy to be recited at special gatherings—or even around watering holes—for generations (cp. 5:10–11). The song focuses on things with which the common people of Israel could identify: the economic hardships of oppression (5:6–7), a call for leadership ("Wake up, wake up, Deborah! "—5:12), the sound of rain and galloping horses (4:21–22), the defeat of a mighty general by the hands of a peasant

The poetry of ancient Israel and its neighbors was characterized by a compositional technique called *parallelism*, where the second of two lines amplifies the first in content, word, or idea. Parallelism can be synonymous (the second line repeats the elements or meaning of the first), antithetic (the second line states the opposite of the first), chiastic (the second line changes the order of elements found in the first), climactic (the second line adds to the elements or meaning of the first), or a combination of these types.

woman (5:24–27), and the longing of a mother for her delayed son (5:28–30). In the end, God's people—His "friends"—rise in glory like the sun (5:31).

The setting of the Gideon story, like that of Israel's victory over Jabin, was the Jezreel Valley. The Jezreel Valley opens up to the hills of Transjordan and the great eastern desert through a relatively narrow passage called Harod Valley, named after the spring of Harod (7:1) located along its southern edge. In times of drought, the peoples of the desert moved into areas that were normally well watered in order to find grazing land for their livestock. The Harod Valley was an inviting doorway that funneled the Midianites into the broad Jezreel basin; the result was similar to the "range wars" between the farmers and ranchers of the old American west.

- *The Song of Deborah provides a valuable*
- *window into the longings and emotions of the*
- *Israelite people when oppressed by their ene-*
- *mies and finally delivered by God. Through*
- *it we can "reach out and touch" Israel in a*
- *way not possible through stories.*

Gideon (6:1–8:35)

Gideon, a peasant farmer of no reputation, led his people to victory against the mighty Midianite hordes. But, the victory "went to his head," and Israel faced a grave threat from within.

The Call of Gideon (6:1–40)

In Jabin, Israel had defeated the power of urban Canaanite civilization. Now their enemy came from the desert, and it was no less formidable. The Midianites, Amalakites, and unnumbered peoples of the East, vast desert hordes, had swarmed into the Jezreel Valley "like swarms of locusts" and stripped the fields bare (6:1, 33). Again Israel cowered, helpless against an enemy (6:6; cp. 5:6–8). The people cried out to God, and God sent a prophet to tell them they were suffering the consequences of their rebellion against Him (6:7–10).

Finally God acted. The angel of the Lord appeared to Gideon, who had been crushed by the Midianite oppression (6:11; cp. 2:1–5). The angel announced to Gideon that he, a "mighty warrior," would lead Israel in battle (6:12).

Gideon was dubious and demanded a sign proving the angel's ability to help (6:13–24).

Gideon began his struggle against Midian by pulling down the local shrine to Baal (6:25–27). The townsmen complained; Baal was, after all, a god of fertility, and when the crops failed he was not to be challenged. Gideon's father came to his defense, arguing that if Baal was a true god, he could take care of himself (6:28–32). The Spirit of the Lord then possessed Gideon and he amassed his army from Manasseh and the tribes of Galilee (6:33–35). Still unsure of success, Gideon asked for two more signs from God (6:36–40).

■ *God chose Gideon, an unlikely young*
■ *farmer, to lead His people to victory.*
■ *Although Gideon doubted his abilities, God*
■ *was patient and brought him to a position*
■ *where he could be used mightily.*

The Defeat of Midian (7:1–25)

Gideon mustered his troops at the spring of Harod, with the hill of Moreh across the valley to the north (7:1). God intended to seize the victory by eliminating any chance for Israel to gain credit through their own efforts (7:2). The soldiers who were afraid were allowed to return home according to a provision in the Mosaic Law (7:3; cp. Deut. 20:8). Of the remainder, only those who drank from the spring in an upright position—cupping the water and raising it to their mouths, thus showing their alertness for battle—were allowed to fight (7:4–7).

On a reconnaissance, Gideon overheard fear in the Midianite camp stemming from a dream

"The Christian's relationship to God as a child to his Father is not only intimate, but sure. So many people seem to do no more than hope for the best; it is possible to know for certain . . . We ought to be sure of our relationship with God not just for the sake of our peace of mind and helpfulness to others, but because God means us to be sure . . . The basis of our knowledge that we are in relationship with God is not our feelings, but the fact that he says we are." John R. W. Stott, *Basic Christianity* (Downers Grove, Ill.: InterVarsity Press, 1958), pp. 132–133.

In the ancient Near East, generals who were preparing for war consulted specialists who could read omens or interpret dreams in order to foresee the outcome of battle. If an omen or a dream was unfavorable, the battle was called off because the troops, believing the omen, would be unfit for battle.

that predicted Israelite victory (7:9–14). Encouraged by the presence of God, Gideon armed his men with only trumpets, torches, and jars, and divided them into three companies surrounding the Midianite camp (7:15–18). At the beginning of the middle watch—when neither the men entering the watch nor those leaving were alert—Gideon's men smashed their jars, waved their torches, and shouted. The Midianites were routed with fear (7:19–23).

Gideon then summoned Israelites from Manasseh, Naphtali, and Asher—the tribes most affected by the Midianite oppression—to join the battle. The fleeing Midianites were choked off in the narrow Harod Valley as they fled eastward toward home. Those who made it to the Jordan River, including the Midianite princes Oreb and Zeeb, were cut down by Ephraimites, who had seized the river's fords (7:24–25).

■ *Gideon's victory over Midian proved again*
■ *the power of God in the midst of human*
■ *weakness. The apostle Paul recalled Jesus'*
■ *answer to his own insufficiencies: "My grace*
■ *is sufficient for you, for my power is made*
■ *perfect in weakness" (2 Cor. 12:9).*

The Troubling Consequences of Victory (8:1–35)

All was not well following Gideon's victory. The Ephraimites were incensed that their role in the battle was not more significant (8:1). Gideon's reply, couched in a proverb, was diplomatic: The real victory was in their killing the Midianite princes (8:2–3). The Ephraimites were satisfied with his answer, but a pattern of tribal infighting had been established (cp. 12:1–6; 20:1–48).

Gideon and his men crossed the Jordan in pursuit of two more Midianite leaders, the kings Zebah and Zalmunna. Gideon asked for provisions from the citizens of Succoth and Penuel, two cities which had been given to the tribe of Gad. The cities refused to help, evidently fearing reprisals from Midian (8:4–9). Years before the men of Gad had helped Joshua conquer Canaan and taken pains to assure the tribes who settled west of the Jordan of their loyalty to all Israel (Josh. 1:12–18; 22:1–34). Now they were concerned only for their own interests. After capturing Zebah and Zalmunna, Gideon returned to Succoth and Penuel and punished their leaders for not giving aid to Israel when asked (8:10–17). He then executed the Midianite kings (8:18–21).

Israel responded to Gideon's resounding victory with pleas for dynastic kingship: "Rule over us, you, your son and your grandson" (8:22). Gideon refused, reminding the people that their only monarch ought to be God (8:23).

Gideon then made an ephod from the gold which he had gathered from his army (8:24–27; cp. Exod. 25:1–9; 35:4–9). The ephod, which should have been located in the tabernacle in Shiloh, became a "snare" for Israel (8:27). Gideon had begun to deliver Israel by tearing down an altar of Baal (6:25–32). He ended his career by building a shrine which rivaled Shiloh and "snared" Israel just as Moses and Joshua had warned that the undefeated Canaanites would do (Exod. 23:32–33; Num. 33:55; Deut. 7:16; Josh. 23:13).

Gideon's victory over Midian entered deeply into the consciousness of the biblical writers. The psalmist cried to God to do to his enemies "as you did to Midian, [and] as you did to Sisera and Jabin at the river Kishon" (Ps. 83:9). In the context of the Messianic announcement of Isaiah 6:9, the prophet Isaiah wrote, "For as in the days of Midian's defeat, you have shattered the yoke that burdens them, the bar across their shoulder, the rod of their oppressor" (Isa. 9:4; cp. Isa. 10:26). Finally, Isaiah saw a day when the Midianites on camels entering Israel would bring not destruction but tribute of gold and frankincense, proclaiming "the praise of the Lord" (Isa. 60:6).

An ephod was a special vestment worn by the high priest containing thread made of finely hammered gold (Exod. 28:4, 31–35; 35:27; 39:2–4, 22–26). The ephod represented the presence of God and intimate access to Him; for this reason, its use was restricted to the high priest. Gideon's ephod may have been such a vestment or a golden image of the person (or deity!) who wore the ephod. In either case, his making an ephod encroached upon areas of authority which were clearly not his.

The story of Gideon ends with an ominous note: Gideon had a son by his concubine from Shechem whom he named Abimelech, "My father is king" (8:29–32). Evidently Israel's wish for a dynasty remained alive. After Gideon died, the people returned to Baal worship (8:33–35). The phrase "and the land had rest" for so many years, which had ended the accounts of the judges prior to Gideon (3:11, 30; 5:31), no longer appears in the book of Judges. A corner had been turned; Israel was about to reap what they had sown.

- *Gideon's work in delivering Israel began to*
- *unravel while he was still alive. Tribal unity*
- *was harder and harder to come by, and God's*
- *ways were easily compromised. Half way*
- *through the period of the judges, Israel's*
- *God-ordained leaders had difficulty remain-*
- *ing faithful to Him. What hope was there for*
- *the people they were to lead?*

ABIMELECH'S ABORTIVE KINGSHIP (9:1–57)

Baal-berith means "covenant Baal," evidently the name of a deity, and the house of Baal-berith was that god's temple. It is unclear whether this deity was an independent god worshiped by the citizens of Shechem or a form of the Lord God corrupted by the Shechemites (cp. Judg. 9:46: El-berith, "covenant God").

Abimelech, Gideon's son (9:1; cp. 6:32), established himself as king in Shechem by turning the political sympathies of its citizens to his own favor (9:1–6). In order to secure his position, he hired a gang of "worthless and reckless fellows" from money given him from the treasury of Shechem stored in the house of Baal-berith. His mercenaries promptly killed all of Gideon's other sons with the exception of Jotham, the youngest, who had hidden himself from the slaughter.

Jotham retreated to Mount Gerazim, the mountain above Shechem on which Israel had recited the blessings of the covenant (Deut. 27:12; Josh. 8:33–34), and shouted a challenge to the men of Shechem in the form of a parable (9:7–21). If they had chosen Abimelech in good faith, then they would live in peace. If, however, they had accepted him as king under less than noble circumstances, they would suffer under his strong arm.

Within three years, Abimelech's tyranny became overbearing, and the region around Shechem was reduced to chaos (9:22–24). Crushed under the iron fist of the son of a mighty judge, the city suffered just as Israel did when there were no judges to deliver them from foreign oppressors (9:25; cp. 5:6–7).

Gaal, a newcomer to Shechem, led an uprising against Abimelech and his deputy-in-charge, Zebul (9:26–30). Gaal's forces were defeated by Abimelech, who then vented his anger by destroying Shechem and its tower (9:31–45). Abimelech fled to Thebez, probably to be identified with Tirzah (1 Kings 16:23), the later Israelite capital six miles northeast of Shechem, and besieged that city. While assaulting the stronghold of Tirzah, Abimelech was killed when a woman dropped an upper millstone weighing several hundred pounds on his head (9:50–54; cp. 2 Sam. 11:21). With the strong man dead, the armies of both sides went home in peace (9:55–57).

Archaeologists have uncovered a strongly fortified "temple tower" near the northern gate in the ruins of Shechem. This tower has been identified as the "tower of Shechem" and the "stronghold of the temple of El Berith" mentioned in Judges 9:46. The city and the temple tower were completely destroyed by a violent conflagration in the mid-12th century B.C., a date which corresponds with the story of Abimelech.

- *In the years following Israel's conquest of*
- *Canaan, God chose to rule His people*
- *directly and raise up judges—deliver-*
- *ers—only when circumstances called for it.*
- *Abimelech usurped God's right to rule and*
- *brought chaos to himself and his people.*

THE LATER JUDGES (10:1–16:31)

The reign of Abimelech was a watershed during the period of the judges. Before his disastrous reign, Israel's judges were concerned primarily with keeping God's covenant; after him, Jephthah and Samson used their position for revenge and personal gain. Slowly but surely each generation added to the sins of the previous generation as Israel slid further and further from God.

Tola and Jair (10:1–5)

The judgeship of Jephthah (10:6–12:7) is framed by a brief mention of the five so-called "minor judges" (10:1–5; 12:8–15). For several reasons, their role in ancient Israel seems to have differed from the other judges:

1. Each is mentioned only briefly in a notation containing primarily genealogical information.
2. Missing is any indication that they led Israel in battle against a foreign enemy.
3. The length of time which each served is given in an exact number of years rather than as a round number.

For these reasons, the work of the minor judges seems to have been more institutional than heroic.

Tola hailed from the tribe of Issachar but lived in the hill country of Ephraim. He judged Israel for 23 years (10:1–2). Jair was from Gilead, a region in the hill country of Transjordan, which was settled by the half-tribe of Manasseh (10:3–5; cp. Josh. 13:29–31). He judged Israel for 22 years.

- *Tola and Jair brought justice to Israel for*
- *over a generation. Although the nature of*
- *their work is largely a matter of speculation,*
- *their service was important enough to war-*
- *rant mention in the Bible. Like the disciples*
- *of Jesus whom we know only by name, these*
- *judges provide an example of quiet but effec-*
- *tive leadership in Israel.*

During the time of the conquest, an Israelite from the tribe of Manasseh named Jair had conquered villages in Transjordan and named them Havvoth Jair ("the tent-villages of Jair") after himself (Deut. 3:14). The Jair of Judges 10:3–5, whose family lived in Havvoth Jair, was evidently a descendant of this man.

Jephthah (10:6–12:7)

Jephthah and his band of mercenaries delivered Israel from an Ammonite invasion. Although he defeated the enemy on the battlefield, he was unable to maintain peace at home.

The Call of Jephthah (10:6–11:11)

Israel again turned from God and fell under the hand of foreign invaders. This time, the enemies were the Philistines on the coast and the Ammonites in Transjordan. The Ammonites crossed the Jordan River and pushed into the central hill country of Israel from the east, while the Philistines moved in from the west. Caught in the middle were the tribes of Judah, Benjamin, and Ephraim (10:6–9).

The people of Israel called out to God but, like the boy who cried wolf, found their pleas unheeded. God's answer was stern: "Go and cry out to the gods you have chosen. Let them save you" (10:10–14). God began to act only after

On their march from the wilderness to the Promised Land, Moses had led the Israelites through Transjordan. As Israel approached the border of Ammon, they were told by God not to fight or take their land, for they were descendants of Lot and, like Israel, they had been given their land by the Lord (Deut. 2:16–22; cp. Gen. 19:36–38).

Israel showed true repentance rather than just lip service (10:15–16).

The leaders of Gilead, the region of Israelite (Manassite) settlement in Transjordan bordering the Ammonites, issued a general call for deliverance, promising that the one who defeated Ammon could rule over them (10:17–18). For Jephthah, a renegade from Gilead who led a band of "worthless fellows" on raids across the desert frontier, this invitation was too good to pass up. Jephthah persuaded the leaders of Gilead to make him their chief *before* going to battle, thereby assuring his position as leader after the crisis had passed (11:1–11).

It was not unusual in antiquity for persons who saw themselves as poor, oppressed, or disenfranchised from society to gather under a charismatic leader and live largely under their own authority, sometimes cooperating with existing authority structures and sometimes opposing them. This tendency for "gang" formation was greatest in times of weakened centralized authority such as the period of the judges. Hence, Abimelech (9:4), Jephthah (11:3), the men attached to Ishbosheth son of Saul (2 Sam. 4:1–3), Jeroboam (2 Chr. 13:6–7), and even David (1 Sam. 22:2) became commanders of bands of men who had withdrawn from society.

- *Jephthah volunteered to deliver Israel from*
- *the Ammonites, provided he could remain the*
- *leader of Gilead. Although God used him,*
- *Jephthah's character was decidedly unlike*
- *that of most judges.*

The Defeat of Ammon (11:12–33)

Jephthah and the king of Ammon squared off in a battle of rhetoric and posturing in a manner characteristic of Near Eastern diplomacy. The Ammonite king claimed that Israel had taken away some of his land when Moses had conquered the Amorite kingdom of Sihon (11:12–13). Jephthah countered that Moses had specifically *not* taken land belonging to Ammon, but that God had given him only the kingdoms of Sihon and Og (11:14–23). Israel was content to dwell in land given them by their God; Ammon should do the same (11:24–27).

After having his message rejected by the king of Ammon, Jephthah attacked. He was empowered by the Spirit of the Lord; evidently God chose to use Jephthah in spite of his faults (11:29). With the power of God behind him, Jephthah's forces easily won the victory (11:32–33).

But all was not well. Jephthah made a vow to God that he would offer as a burnt offering the first person who would greet him at his own doors if he was victorious in battle (11:30–31). His vow was rash—but not entirely unexpected for a man whose life was characterized by big talk.

- *Jephthah was chosen by God to deliver Israel*
- *from foreign oppression, even though Israel*
- *did not deserve to be delivered and Jephthah*
- *did not deserve to be used. Sometimes God's*
- *ways are difficult to understand, but His pur-*
- *poses always prevail.*

The Troubling Consequences of Victory (11:34–12:7)

When Jephthah arrived home, he was met at the door by his daughter, his only child, who danced with joy at her father's return (11:34). Jephthah was overcome with remorse, but he never considered reneging on his vow to offer her as a burnt offering to God (11:35). Tragically, his daughter was compliant. After "bewailing her virginity" with her friends, Jephthah "did to her as he had vowed" (11:36–39).

Jephthah's brutal actions caused consternation in Israel (11:40) as they continue to do for Bible readers today. Not willing to accept the act of

Bible readers sometimes confuse the Amorites and the Ammonites. "Amorite" is a generic term for any person indigenous to Canaan and Transjordan or, more particularly, anyone living in the hill country (cp. Gen. 15:16; Num. 13:29). The Ammonites were a specific Old Testament nation living in and around the city of Rabbath-ammon (modern Amman, Jordan), high in the hill country of Transjordan.

Chemosh was the god of the Moabites, Ammon's neighbor to the south (Num. 21:29; 1 Kings 11:7; Jer. 48:46). His name is found twelve times on the Mesha Stele, a Moabite inscription dating to the years immediately following the death of Ahab which was found in 1868 in the city of Dibon east of the Dead Sea. Jephthah probably mentioned Chemosh in connection with the Ammonites because the cities which the Ammonite king was trying to seize were also claimed by Moab (Judg. 11:26).

human sacrifice, some interpreters suggest that Jephthah only prevented his daughter from marrying, effectively ending her life in the culture of the day (11:38–40). The text is unclear as to the exact outcome of Jephthah's actions, perhaps because the writer himself was too overcome by the facts of the case to be more explicit.

After the Ammonites had been defeated, the Ephraimites crossed the Jordan River and confronted Jephthah about not being allowed to participate in the battle (12:1). The Ephraimites evidently thought themselves the dominant tribe and were unwilling for others to do "their" job in protecting Israel (see 12:4). When Gideon fought the Midianites, the Ephraimites had voiced similar complaints (8:1–3), but this time they were ready to fight for what they saw as their right. Jephthah's reply, defensive as always, was that Ephraim *had* received the chance to deliver Israel from Ammon but failed to act (cp. 10:9, 18); by implication, Jephthah said that he had delivered Israel only because no one else was willing to do so.

The Hebrew word *shibboleth* means "ear of grain" or "flowing torrent," the latter a more appropriate meaning in the context of Judges 12:5. Some scholars have argued from linguistic evidence that the Gileadites actually pronounced the word *thibboleth* and the Ephraimites said *shibboleth*. In either case, this and other evidence shows that dialectical differences were present in the Hebrew of ancient Israel.

Insulted, Jephthah and his band fought against Ephraim and defeated them (12:4). The Ephraimites turned back to flee across the Jordan, but Jephthah's men had seized the natural crossing points along the river. There they used a linguistic test to determine which of the men crossing the Jordan were escaping Ephraimites (12:5–6). The local speech patterns of the Israelites had begun to change as the various tribes settled into their own homes throughout Canaan. One of these changes was that the Ephraimites lost the "sh" sound and replaced it with "s," with the result that they pronounced *shibboleth* with an accent.

- *God provided the victory, but His people*
- *marred the consequences. The career of Jeph-*
- *thah illustrates the natural tendency of peo-*
- *ple to look after their own interests. With*
- *each person looking out for himself, the foun-*
- *dation blocks of Israelite society began to*
- *crumble.*

Ibzan, Elon, and Abdon (12:8–15)

The record of three more "minor judges" follows the Jephthah story (cp. 10:1–5). Ibzan was from Bethlehem, probably the Bethlehem located in the tribal inheritance of Zebulun (cp. Josh. 19:15) about seven miles west of the place where, centuries later, the village of Nazareth would be settled. Although some scholars have tried to argue that Bethlehem of Zebulun was the birthplace of Jesus, the Gospels are quite clear that Jesus, the descendant of David, was born in Bethlehem of Judah, David's city (cp. Matt. 2:1–6; Luke 2:4). Ibzan judged Israel for seven years.

Elon, who judged Israel for ten years, was also from the tribe of Zebulun (12:11–12). Abdon was a Pirathonite—an inhabitant of Pirathon in the hill country of Ephraim (12:13–15). His identity was found not in a tribe but in a local clan, evidence of the breakdown of tribal unity during the period of the judges. Like Ibzan (12:8–9) and Jair (10:4), Abdon was evidently a man of wealth. He judged Israel for eight years.

In tribal society, allegiance was first to one's family, then to one's extended family or clan, next to one's tribe, and finally to one's nation—if one existed. Personal identity was thus fluid, depending on the particular situation—or enemy—at hand. Except for the judgeship of Othniel (3:7–11), tribal unity was impossible to maintain during the time of the judges.

■ *The accounts of Ibzan, Elon, and Abdon pro-*
■ *vide a brief respite in Israel's downward spi-*
■ *ral during the days of the judges.*

Samson (13:1–16:31)

The last deliverer of Israel whose story is recorded in the book of Judges was Samson, a man whose powerful physique and strong passions led him into a titan clash with the Philistines. Samson's career as a judge was characterized by personal revenge and counter-revenge, yet he was used by God to check the Philistine advance into the hill country of Israel.

The Announcement and Birth of Samson (13:1–25)

The Samson story begins with the refrain familiar to the reader of Judges: "Again the Israelites did evil in the eyes of the Lord" (13:1). This time the enemy who oppressed Israel was the Philistines, a people who would become Israel's great enemy during the formation of the monarchy under Saul and David.

The Samson story gives detailed attention to circumstances surrounding his birth. The angel of the Lord appeared to a certain Manoah and his barren wife, a couple from the tribe of Dan (13:2; cp. 2:1; 6:12). They were to have a child who was to be a Nazirite, one consecrated to God from birth. The child was not to cut his hair—thus wearing for all to see his special role for God—nor was he to eat and drink things inappropriate for priests (13:3–7). Manoah begged to be given instructions for raising such a special child, but was told only to see that his

The Philistines lived along the coastal plain of southern Canaan, generally from Joppa (modern Tel Aviv) to Gaza. The word *Palestine* comes from Philistia, the name given their homeland. Historical evidence attests to the arrival of various people groups (called "Sea People") from the islands of the Aegean and surrounding lands who settled along the eastern Mediterranean coast during the centuries that Israel was settling the hill country of Canaan. It was inevitable that the two emerging nations would clash. The Philistines established a pentapolis of confederated cities: Gaza, Ashkelon, Ashdod, Ekron, and Gath (Josh. 11:22; 1 Sam. 6:17).

son remained a Nazirite (13:8–14). The angel disappeared in a flame to heaven, leaving Manoah and his wife awestruck with fear (13:15–23).

True to the divine word, Manoah's wife gave birth to a son whom she named Samson, a derivation of the Hebrew word *sun* (13:24–25). The boy grew, God blessed him, and "the Spirit of the Lord began to stir him" for action.

■ *The book of Judges reaches a climax with the*
■ *career of Samson. Samson's birth was mirac-*
■ *ulous. As a Nazirite, his life was to be special*
■ *before God and Israel. The anticipation that*
■ *someone would finally break the cycle of*
■ *oppression that had troubled Israel was great.*
■ *But would Samson live up to his calling?*

Samson's Struggle with the Philistines (14:1–16:3)

Samson grew up in the Sorek Valley (cp. 16:4). At its eastern end, as the valley entered the hill country which was settled by the tribe of Dan, were Zorah and Eshtaol, Samson's hometowns (13:25; cp. 16:31). At its western end, where the valley emptied onto the coastal plain, lived the Philistines. Midway between the two was the city of Timnah, where Samson journeyed one day and fell in love with a young Philistine woman (14:1–3). Although marriage to a non-Israelite was anathema for a Nazirite, God used Samson's passions to begin the process by which He checked the Philistine domination of Israel (14:4).

"Nazirite" comes from a Hebrew word (*nazir*) that means "consecrated one." The Nazirites were persons dedicated to God by means of a vow. They expressed their devotion by eating special foods and not cutting their hair. Although the origins of the Nazirites are unknown, they were given legal status in Numbers 6:1–21. The word *Nazirite* must not be confused with "Nazarene," a term used to designate Jesus and His followers (see Matt. 2:23). A Nazarene was an inhabitant of Nazareth, a name that comes from a Hebrew word meaning "branch" or "shoot" and is unrelated to the word "Nazirite." Nevertheless, the angel's annunciation to Manoah and his wife has interesting parallels to the annunciation of Jesus' birth (Luke 1:26–38).

Samson sought, and evidently gained, parental approval for his marriage to the Philistine woman (14:5, 10). He gave a great feast for the people of Timnah—evidently his wedding feast (14:10; cp. v. 15)—and challenged the guests to a match of wits. If they could guess his riddle—an impossibility, for it was based on something which he had done in secret (14:5–9)—then he would reward them with fine clothing for thirty people; if not, they would provide the same for him (14:10–14).

The men of Timnah were desperate, and they forced Samson's new wife to entice the answer from him (14:15). Her loyalties were first to her people, and Samson could not resist the pleas of a pretty woman (14:16–17). When Samson's riddle was answered, he became indignant. Empowered by the Spirit of the Lord, Samson killed thirty Philistines in Ashkelon, a city deep in Philistia, and gave their clothing to the men of Timnah (14:18–19). He went home, and his wife was given to his best man (14:20).

When Samson heard that his wife had been taken from him, he reacted with revenge. He caught three hundred foxes, set fire to their tails and set them loose in the Philistines' grain fields (15:1–5). The Philistines in turn killed Samson's wife (15:6). He struck back and slaughtered many of them, then fled, exhausted and ready for a truce, to the rock Etam, a stronghold deep in the Judean hills near Bethlehem (15:7–8).

The Philistines pushed into the hill country to pressure Judah into turning Samson over to them (15:9–10). Fearing more Philistine reprisals, the men of Judah complied (15:11). Samson, again seeking an opportunity to defeat the Philistines, allowed himself to be tied with ropes and led to the Philistines. Then he broke his bonds and killed them with a donkey's jawbone (15:12–17).

Samson's next exploit took him all the way to Gaza, the Philistine city the greatest distance from his home, where he spent the night with a prostitute (16:1). Thinking they had him at last, the Philistines barred the city gate and lay in wait (16:2). Samson pulled the gate from the city wall and carried it on his back to Hebron. This was a forty-mile hike ending in a rugged three-thousand-foot climb (16:3). The most secure Philistine city now lay open to anyone.

The writer of Judges was careful to note that Samson was chosen and empowered by God to fight against the Philistines (13:3–5, 25; 14:4, 19; 15:14). Samson was given every opportunity to succeed in his struggles against the Philistines *and* be a holy man of God. Yet his actions seem to be those of a man of extreme passion who was bent on revenge against anyone who might cross his path.

It is difficult to understand how God could use a man who had as many character flaws as Samson. Perhaps God's purposes for Israel, given the time and circumstances, could best be fulfilled not by an all-out war against the Philistines but by the hit-and-run tactics of an individual. Samson could infiltrate the Philistine cities, hit them from behind, and withdraw, disrupting the Philistine advance against Israel. Ultimately all we can say is that God is sovereign and uses whomever He will to do His will, and some—like Samson—in spite of themselves.

Samson's weapons were nontraditional: fiery foxes (15:4–5), a donkey's jawbone (15:15), and his own two hands (14:6; 16:3, 29). Why Samson did not use a sword or spear may be explained in part by the Philistine monopoly on metalworking (1 Sam. 13:19–22). When David battled the Philistine Goliath he also carried a weapon with no metal (1 Sam. 17:40 43).

■ *Samson was able to bring havoc upon the*
■ *cities and villages of the Philistines. His*
■ *exploits were heroic, but they seemed to stir*
■ *up more trouble than they solved. God used*
■ *Samson, just like He uses us, but it is also our*
■ *responsibility, as it was Samson's, to become*
■ *vessels worthy of His honor.*

Samson and Delilah (16:4–31)

Samson's exploits ended where they began—with a stroll down the Sorek Valley and an encounter with a Philistine woman (16:4; cp. 14:1). The Philistines enticed Delilah, who was possibly Samson's wife—although this is not explicitly stated in the text—to find out for them the secret of his great strength. For this task, she accepted 1,100 pieces of silver, a sum which figures into an unrelated story that follows (cp. 17:2).

Delilah used all the seductive cunning, patience, and wit she could muster to coax Samson's secret from him. Samson toyed with Delilah, pretending to tell while all the while making the Philistines—and Delilah—look like fools (16:6–15). The story is told in an entertaining, suspenseful way, leaving the reader to wonder if Samson might finally do himself in. Finally, Samson revealed the secret of his Nazirite vow—a claim which, owing to Samson's reputation for wild living, must have been as unbelievable to Delilah as everything else he had told her (16:16–17). She nevertheless shaved his head—and he was promptly captured, blinded, and taken to a Gaza prison to grind grain like an animal in the mill (16:18–21). The Lord had finally left him, and Samson's weaknesses, no longer covered up by God, must have surprised himself most of all.

In prison, Samson's hair began to grow, a hint for the reader that he was not yet defeated (16:22). He was taken from prison to perform for the Philistines at a festival in the temple of Dagon, the god of grain (16:23–27). A life of violence often ends in violence, and Samson prayed for one last act of revenge. He pushed against the temple's supporting pillars—and brought the whole thing down on his head, killing more Philistines in his own death than he had during his life (16:28–30). Samson was buried in his hometown of Eshtaol (16:31; cp. 13:25). With Samson's death, the Philistines were given free reign to encroach into the Israelite hill country, setting the political and military stage for the book of 1 Samuel (cp. 1 Sam. 4:1–7:14; 9:15–16; 13:2–14:52; 17:1–58; 23:1–5; 28:1–29:11; 31:1–13).

Archaeological excavations at Tell Qasile, the site of a Philistine city near modern Tel Aviv, uncovered a small temple dedicated to a Philistine deity. This is the only Philistine religious center found to date. The roof of the main hall was supported by two stone pillars about six feet apart, and the walls were lined with benches. It is thought that the temple of Dagon in Gaza was of this type.

■ *Samson was able to check the Philistines but*
■ *not to defeat them, and his actions as judge*
■ *showed that Israel needed "something else."*
■ *In the end, the judges were unable to keep*
■ *Israel's enemies at bay—no doubt, according*
■ *to the writer of Judges—because they were*
■ *also unable to keep God's covenant.*

QUESTIONS TO GUIDE YOUR STUDY

1. Describe the cycle of sin and deliverance in the book of Judges. What evidence is there that this cycle spiraled *downward*?

2. Did the judges act according to God's will, or just according to His plan? What's the difference?

3. How does God use unexpected people to do His work today?

THE PERIOD OF THE JUDGES: ISRAEL'S DOMESTIC AFFAIRS (17:1–21:25)

The exploits of the various judges show that Israel was generally able to counter foreign oppression. But the last two stories in the book of Judges proved Israel's inability to establish a just and righteous society at home. Having forsaken God, Israel was left without effective leadership. The results were disastrous: The tribe of Dan abandoned their inheritance for greener pastures, and the tribe of Benjamin was decimated by an Israelite civil war. These stories are held together by the refrain, "Everyone did as he saw fit" (17:6; 21:25), an honest assessment of the tragic state into which Israel had fallen.

THE MIGRATION OF THE TRIBE OF DAN (17:1–18:31)

The story of the migration of Dan illustrates the lack of restraint in Israel during the period of the judges.

Micah and His Idolatrous Priest (17:1–13)

The story of the relocation of Dan begins abruptly with an episode providing background information for the main narrative of chapter 18.

Micah, an Ephraimite, confessed to stealing a vast sum of money—1,100 pieces of silver—from his own mother (17:1–2). The theft is not explained, nor is the origin of so large a hoard (but cp. 16:5). Micah's mother responded by overlooking his crime and dedicating the money to the Lord—so that her son could make from it a graven image (17:3–4). Micah established his own worship center complete with an idol (teraphim), an ephod (cp. 8:27), and his own son as priest (17:5).

Years before, Moses had commanded Israel to remain faithful to God by passing his word from one generation to the next (Deut. 6:6–7). Micah and his mother were oblivious to that parental responsibility (cp. 2:10). Israel's ways had become virtually indistinguishable from the Canaanites.

Into Micah's world walked a Levitical priest from Bethlehem, set on finding fame and fortune (17:7–9). Micah installed him as priest in his local shrine, apparently reasoning that in matters of the divine, a renegade Levite was better than one's own son. Now that his shrine was "legitimate," he reasoned, God had to bless him (17:10–13).

An ephod was a special garment worn by the high priest which represented the presence of God and the possibility of intimate access to Him. The teraphim were small household idols (cp. Gen. 31:19). Many teraphim have been found in archaeological excavations throughout Israel. The ephod and teraphim were commonly used in ancient Near Eastern religions for divination—attempts to foretell the future by cajoling and manipulating the deities to which they were dedicated.

■ *Micah and a Levitical priest decided to estab-*
■ *lish their own shrine in the hill country of*
■ *Ephraim. This act showed they had suc-*
■ *cumbed to the ways of the Canaanites. Israel*
■ *was no longer a distinctive people of God;*
■ *they had become just another people search-*
■ *ing for God.*

The Relocation of Dan (18:1–31)

The story continues with a shift of scene. The opening verse of chapter 18 states that the tribe of Dan was seeking an inheritance within Canaan. This does not mean that the events in chapter 18 took place before Joshua allotted Dan its land bordering the region of the Philistines (Josh. 19:40–48), but only that Dan was unable to secure and hold its land against foreign oppression (cp. 1:34; 13:1; 14:4). Rather than face the Philistine threat, Dan decided to look for safer pastures elsewhere.

The Danites sent out spies (cp. Num. 13:2, 17–20; Josh. 2:1) from Zorah and Eshtaol, Samson's hometowns (cp. 13:25; 16:31), to explore the land of Canaan (18:2). They came to the house of Micah and received word from his priest, evidently through divination (cp. 17:5, 12), that their journey would succeed (18:3–6). The spies continued all the way to Laish, where the people were "unsuspecting and secure" (18:7). This city was north of Hazor at the edge of the tribal inheritance of Naphtali.

The city of Laish, biblical Dan, was located at the foot of Mount Hermon next to a powerful spring which forms the headwaters of the Jordan River. This lush area serves as the northern gateway into Israel. Laish was a major Canaanite city during the time of the patriarchs and was probably visited by Abraham on his journey into the land (Gen. 12:1–6; cp. 14:14). Archaeological excavations at Laish/ Dan have uncovered evidence of close economic and cultural ties to Crete and Phoenicia, illustrating the claim of Judges 18:7 that its citizens lived like the Sidonians and were prosperous.

The spies returned home and reported that God was giving them a new land where "unsuspecting" people—rather than troublesome Philistines—lived (18:8–10). The Danites formed an army and set out to conquer Laish for themselves (18:11–13). They stopped at the home of Micah and procured his priest and religious paraphernalia; the priest readily agreed to go after being told by the Danites that working for a tribe was a promotion he couldn't pass up (18:14–20). Micah was understandably upset, but he stood helpless before the Danites' show of force (18:21–26).

The Danites arrived at Laish—again described as "peaceful and unsuspecting" (18:27)—killed its inhabitants, and burned the city. They renamed the city "Dan," set up the idol they had stolen from Micah, and installed the kidnapped Levitical priest to serve there (18:28–31). As an important historic note, the writer mentioned that the priest was none other than the grandson of Moses (18:30).

The story of the relocation of the tribe of Dan is told in a way that brings shame to the Northern Kingdom of Israel. When the Israelite monarchy split between north and south, Jeroboam established religious centers at Bethel, the kingdom's southernmost city, and Dan (1 Kings 12:25–33), in an attempt—largely successful, it turned out—to pull his people away from Jerusalem. The episode recorded in Judges 18 shows that Jeroboam added to an aberrant religious tradition that was already present at Dan. The Danites claimed to have God's blessing (18:10), and their work seemed to gain legitimacy because their Levitical priest was a direct descendant of Moses. Yet the entire endeavor was characterized by ill intent, theft, corruption, and faithlessness at all levels of society.

The writers of the Old Testament described the traditional borders of the land of Israel before the time of the divided monarchy with the phrase "from Dan to Beersheba" (Judg. 20:1; 2 Sam. 3:10; 17:11; 24:2; 1 Kings 4:25; 2 Chr. 30:5). These were the northern and southernmost cities, respectively, of the united monarchy. The phrase "the people of Israel from Dan to Beersheba" means "all Israel."

■ *The story of the relocation of the tribe of Dan*
■ *provides an important backdrop to the "sins*
■ *of Jeroboam" (cp. 1 Kings 14:16; 2 Kings*
■ *15:28) that plagued Israel during the monar-*
■ *chy. The effective leadership that Israel*
■ *enjoyed under Moses and Joshua had com-*
■ *pletely disappeared. Lacking a king (17:6;*
■ *18:1) and being led by a corrupted priest-*
■ *hood based in a rival sanctuary (18:30–31),*
■ *Israel was indeed in desperate straits.*

CIVIL WAR IN ISRAEL (19:1–21:25)

The final story in Judges brings to a climax the horrible conditions that prevailed in Israel during the days before the rise of the monarchy. Israel had no king—but they also refused to follow God. Their emerging nation was leaderless, and chaos was the result.

The Levite's journey from Bethlehem to his home in the hill country of Ephraim took him along the main north-south route in the hill country of Israel. The route followed the watershed line and so passed by, but did not go into, Jebus (cp. 19:10). Jebus was the pre-Israelite name of Jerusalem. The city of Jebus, situated on a low spur which extends southward from the present walled city of Jerusalem, was separated from the watershed ridge by two valleys (the Hinnom and Tyropoean Valleys) and a hill which is today called Mount Zion.

Gibeah was the hometown of Saul, son of Kish, who became the first king of Israel (1 Sam. 9:1–2; 10:26).

The Rape of the Levite's Concubine (19:1–30)

The Israelite civil war began, as wars often do, with everyday events caused by normal people. The story opens with a Levite from Ephraim—and, remembering the character flaws of the Levite in the preceding story, the reader is led to expect only the worse. The Levite took a concubine from Bethlehem, but she became angry and returned home (19:1–2). After a time, he followed her and convinced her to go back with him (19:3). His return was delayed and when the small party finally left Bethlehem, the day was already late (19:4–9). Bypassing Jebus (Jerusalem) because the city was still Canaanite and thus unable to provide suitable lodging for a priest, the Levite and his concubine stopped at Gibeah, the next town north (19:10–14).

The Levite and his concubine were not invited into anyone's home for the night—a serious breach of Near Eastern etiquette (19:15). Finally, a lone old farmer extended them the expected courtesy (19:16–21). That night the men of the city—"wicked men" they are called—beat down his door with the intent of forcing homosexual relations with the Levite. The old man refused, offering his own virgin daughter and the Levite's concubine instead. To avoid a riot, the Levite pushed his concubine out the door where she was gang raped all night and finally fell, dead, onto her master's doorstep (19:22–26).

The Levite evidently slept well. The next morning he was surprised to find his concubine dead (19:27–28). He took her home, dismembered her lifeless body, and sent the pieces to each of the twelve tribes (19:29). His act was symbolic. If Israel failed to help him take revenge, they would suffer the same fate as his concubine (cp. 1 Sam. 11:6–7)

The reaction throughout Israel was uniform: "Such a thing has never been seen or done" (19:30). Their response, however, was appropriately imprecise: The "such a thing" had in mind the behavior of the men of Gibeah—and of the Levite.

■ *With the rape of the Levite's concubine, the*
■ *moral depravity of Israel reached a new low.*
■ *Israel was appalled at the act, but would*
■ *their solution solve the problem or add to it?*

The Defeat of the Tribe of Benjamin (20:1–48)

In answer to the call of the Levite, the people of Israel and their tribal leaders assembled at Mizpah, a city in Benjamin five miles north of Gibeah (20:1–2). Their intent was to take official action against the men of Gibeah. When asked what had happened, the Levite condemned the men, but exonerated himself: "The men of Gibeah came after me and surrounded the house, intending to kill me," he said. "They raped my concubine, and she died" (20:3–7). The Levite, of course, said nothing about his own complicity in the tragedy (cp. 19:25, 27–28).

Israel resolved to fight Benjamin "as one man" (20:8–11). This phrase is unexpected, given the disunity which had characterized Israel during the time of the judges. It is ironic that in the last episode of the book, all Israel finally came together—but to fight against one of their own tribes, not a foreign oppressor.

The men of Sodom attempted to engage in homosexual acts with Lot's male guests (hence, "sodomy"), but were prevented from doing so by God (Gen. 19:4–11). Because such activity was characteristic of the inhabitants of Sodom, God destroyed the city (Gen. 19:12–28). The story of the Levite's concubine is clearly intended to identify the men of Gibeah as no better than the Sodomites.

The writer of Judges mentioned seven hundred left-handed slingers from Benjamin (20:16). Evidently the tribe of Benjamin gained a reputation for having skilled left-handed warriors. Ehud, the judge from Benjamin, was left-handed (Judg. 3:15, 21) as were a special Benjaminite contingent of David's soldiers (1 Chr. 12:1–2). Biblical notes such as these help give the Bible a "real life" flavor and make its reading more enjoyable.

The sling was a common weapon in ancient warfare. The use of a sling increased the range of a thrown stone. Ancient Egyptian and Assyrian reliefs show slingers and archers standing together as long-range attackers. On several occasions the Bible makes specific mention of slingers in battle, the best known being David's fight against Goliath (Judg. 20:16; 1 Sam. 17:48–50; 2 Kings 3:25; 1 Chr. 12:1–2; 2 Chr. 26:14).

The Benjaminites refused to turn the men who had committed the gang rape over to the Israelite force for punishment (20:12–13). By their refusal, the entire tribe became implicated in the crime. What was worse, they decided to fight against Israel in order to protect the criminals (20:14–17).

Faced with war, the Israelites asked God which tribe should fight against Benjamin first. The reply was "Judah," but the actual account of battle mentions only Israel (20:18; cp. vv. 19; 1:1–2). It is difficult to know if Judah simply took a position of leadership or if they alone fought Benjamin; the former is more likely.

Twice Israel attacked, and twice they were beaten by the smaller yet superior Benjaminite force (20:19–25). Before each battle, God had told Israel to fight against Benjamin (20:18, 23); the third time He added that they would win (20:28).

Israel finally set up an ambush against Gibeah much the same way as Joshua had done against Ai (20:29; cp. Josh. 8:3–23). A small contingent of Israelites drew the Benjaminites out of their city by pretending to be beaten before them; the main Israelite force swept in from behind and annihilated the Benjaminite army (20:30–36).

The account of the battle at Gibeah ends with a detailed retelling of certain elements of the fight (20:36–48). The Benjaminites fled from the slaughter northeast toward the wilderness, where only six hundred found refuge at the rock of Rimmon (20:43–47). Gibeah and the surrounding towns were destroyed with fire (20:40, 48).

- Israel was drawn into civil war by the rape
- of the Levite's concubine. The entire tribe of
- Benjamin paid dearly for supporting the
- criminal actions of a few.

The Troubling Consequences of . . . Victory? (21:1–25)

The tribe of Benjamin was decimated by the civil war. Israel had won, but the victory was hollow. There were not enough women left in Benjamin to ensure the tribe's survival into the next generation. What was worse, before the battle had begun Israel had taken a vow that anyone who gave his daughter as wife to a Benjaminite would be killed (21:1, 5). Up to this point, such a blanket prohibition on marriage had applied only to the Canaanites (cp. Deut. 7:3). The war had begun with a dismembered concubine; with Benjamin defeated, Israel itself had become dismembered (21:3).

The tribes met to discuss how Benjamin might be restored. They asked God why "this" had come to pass—perhaps an innocent question but odd nonetheless since they themselves were party to Benjamin's demise (21:3–4). No answer from God is recorded, but the Israelites decided to take action anyway. It was resolved that wives from Benjamin should be taken from Jabesh-gilead, a city of Manasseh in Transjordan. The men of Jabesh-gilead would be killed for not joining the battle against Benjamin and their widows would be given to the men of Benjamin who had lost their wives in the civil war (21:5–12). In this way, Israel could fulfill its vow under the guise of punishing a noncooperative city. Clearly, this vow was as rash as that of

The ark of the covenant played a dominant role in the early part of the book of Joshua as Israel crossed from the wilderness into Canaan (Josh. 3:1–6:21). It was present in Shechem when Joshua and Israel renewed the covenant there (Josh. 8:30–35). In 1 Samuel the ark was located in Shiloh (1 Sam. 3:3), the city from which Joshua had apportioned the tribal inheritances to Israel. However, the ark is mentioned only once in Judges, and that in an incidental note commenting that at the time it was located in Bethel (20:27–28, cp. v. 18). The absence of the ark in the narratives of Judges reflects the moral decline of the Israelites during that period.

Jephthah, and the consequences just as shocking (cp. 11:30–31, 34–40).

With their husbands now dead ostensibly for other reasons, the Jabesh Gilead widows were free to marry the Benjaminites, who were taking refuge at the rock of Rimmon (21:13–15). The need for wives, however, was not fully met, so a second solution was proposed. It was suggested that the Benjaminites be allowed to kidnap young women who were celebrating at a yearly feast in Shiloh (21:16–22). Again, the vow would not be broken because the women would not actually be *given* in marriage. The Benjaminites readily agreed, and their tribe was slowly rebuilt (21:23).

The last two verses of Judges summarize the unstable condition of Israel in the years before the rise of the monarchy. On the one hand, Judges 21:24 presents a quiet picture, with each Israelite living on his own land and enjoying the fruit of his labor. The book of Joshua ended much the same way (Josh. 24:28). However, Judges 21:25 gives the final word. Each Israelite *was* living on his own land, but he was also doing whatever seemed right to him. It was as if there were no nation, no tribe, no clan, or no family—just a mass of individuals each pulling in whatever direction they wished.

The term translated "yearly festival" (Hebrew *hag*) in Judges 21:19 is used in the Old Testament to refer to Israel's three great pilgrimage festivals: Passover, the Feast of Weeks (Shavuot), and the Feast of Tabernacles (Sukkot) (Deut. 16:1–17). The nature of the festival in Judges 21, however, seems to be different. Because of the dancing maidens, some interpreters have connected it to an annual festival celebrating the grape harvest. The yearly trip which Hannah and her husband made to Shiloh may or may not be related to this festival (1 Sam. 1:3; 2:19).

■ *The book of Judges ends in despair. People,*
■ *acting without God, find their own solutions,*
■ *but those solutions are sometimes worse than*
■ *the initial problem. A single act—the horri-*
■ *ble violation of an innocent woman*
■ *(19:25)—led to untold suffering by thou-*
■ *sands. Israel had wandered so far from God*
■ *that they failed to recognize where they*
■ *could find the proper solution for their*
■ *problems.*

QUESTIONS TO GUIDE YOUR STUDY

1. What lessons does the book of Judges teach about problem solving?
2. When read in light of Joshua 21, how does Judges 17–19 show that the priests were largely responsible for the woeful state into which Israel had fallen during the time of the judges?
3. How do the last five chapters of Judges serve as a bridge to the period of the monarchy?

* * * * * *

At the beginning of the book of Joshua, Israel was one people, united in vision and spirit. The unifying factor was God's covenant. Each Israelite pledged his or her loyalty to the covenant and readily submitted to their leaders, men who were capable not just to lead, but to lead *righteously*. By the end of the book of Judges, Israel had fractured into countless pieces. The solution, the writer of Judges hinted, was a king (17:6; 18:1; 19:1; 21:25).

Judges was probably written during the early part of the monarchy, after God had reestablished his covenant with David (cp. 2 Sam. 7:4–16; 2 Sam. 23:5). Under David, the covenant would again become the unifying force within Israel, but this time it would be expressed through kingship and the Temple. With the close of Judges, a new day was about to dawn; the darkness of night was about to give way to a new kind of light.

* * * * * *

The following is a collection of Broadman & Holman published reference sources used for this work. They are provided here to meet the reader's need for more specific information and/or an expanded treatment of the books of Joshua and Judges. All of these works will greatly aid in the reader's study, teaching, and presentation of Joshua and Judges. The accompanying annotations can be helpful in guiding the reader to the proper resources.

Cate, Robert L. *An Introduction to the Historical Books of the Old Testament.* A survey of the books of Joshua through Esther with special attention to issues of history writing in ancient Israel.

Cate, Robert L. *An Introduction to the Old Testament and Its Study.* An introductory work presenting background information, issues related to interpretation, and summaries of each book of the Old Testament.

Dockery, David S., Kenneth A. Mathews and Robert B. Sloan. *Foundations for Biblical Interpretation: A Complete Library of Tools and Resources.* A comprehensive introduction to matters relating to the composition and interpretation of the entire Bible. This work includes a discussion of the geographical, historical, cultural, religious, and political backgrounds of the Bible.

Farris, T. V. *Mighty to Save: A Study in Old Testament Soteriology.* A wonderful evaluation of many Old Testament passages that teach about salvation. This work makes a conscious attempt to apply Old Testament teachings to the Christian life.

Francisco, Clyde T. *Introducing the Old Testament.* Revised edition. An introductory guide to each of the books of the Old Testament. This work includes a discussion on how to interpret the Old Testament.

Holman Bible Dictionary. An exhaustive, alphabetically arranged resource of Bible-related subjects. An excellent tool of definitions and other information on the people, places, things, and events of the books of Joshua and Judges.

Holman Bible Handbook. A summary treatment of each book of the Bible that offers outlines, commentary on key themes and sections, illustrations, charts, maps, and full-color photos. This tool also provides an accent on broader theological teachings of the Bible.

Holman Book of Biblical Charts, Maps, and Reconstructions. This easy-to-use work provides numerous color charts on various matters related to Bible content and background, maps of important events, and drawings of objects, buildings, and cities mentioned in the Bible.

Kent, Dan G. *Joshua, Judges, Ruth.* (Layman's Bible Book Commentary, vol. 4). A popular-level treatment of the books of Joshua, Judges, and Ruth. This easy-to-use volume provides a relevant and practical perspective for the reader.

Sandy, D. Brent and Ronald L. Giese, Jr. *Cracking Old Testament Codes. A Guide to Interpreting the Literary Genres of the Old Testament.* This book is designed to make scholarly discussions available to preachers and teachers.

Smith, Ralph L. *Old Testament Theology: Its History, Method and Message.* A comprehensive treatment of various issues relating to Old Testament theology. Written for university and seminary students, ministers, and advanced lay teachers.

SHEPHERD'S NOTES

SHEPHERD'S NOTES